WOOTTON

THE RAF AT WAR

Other Publications:

PLANET EARTH
COLLECTOR'S LIBRARY OF THE CIVIL WAR
LIBRARY OF HEALTH
CLASSICS OF THE OLD WEST
THE GOOD COOK
THE SEAFARERS
THE ENCYCLOPEDIA OF COLLECTIBLES
THE GREAT CITIES
WORLD WAR II
HOME REPAIR AND IMPROVEMENT
THE WORLD'S WILD PLACES
THE TIME-LIFE LIBRARY OF BOATING
HUMAN BEHAVIOR
THE ART OF SEWING
THE OLD WEST
THE EMERGENCE OF MAN
THE AMERICAN WILDERNESS
THE TIME-LIFE ENCYCLOPEDIA OF GARDENING
LIFE LIBRARY OF PHOTOGRAPHY
THIS FABULOUS CENTURY
FOODS OF THE WORLD
TIME-LIFE LIBRARY OF AMERICA
TIME-LIFE LIBRARY OF ART
GREAT AGES OF MAN
LIFE SCIENCE LIBRARY
THE LIFE HISTORY OF THE UNITED STATES
TIME READING PROGRAM
LIFE NATURE LIBRARY
LIFE WORLD LIBRARY

FAMILY LIBRARY:
HOW THINGS WORK IN YOUR HOME
THE TIME-LIFE BOOK OF THE FAMILY CAR
THE TIME-LIFE FAMILY LEGAL GUIDE
THE TIME-LIFE BOOK OF FAMILY FINANCE

This volume is one of a series that traces the adventure and science of aviation, from the earliest manned balloon ascension through the era of jet flight.

THE RAF AT WAR

by Ralph Barker

AND THE EDITORS OF TIME-LIFE BOOKS

TIME-LIFE BOOKS, ALEXANDRIA, VIRGINIA

Time-Life Books Inc.
is a wholly owned subsidiary of

TIME INCORPORATED

FOUNDER: Henry R. Luce 1898-1967

Editor-in-Chief: Henry Anatole Grunwald
President: J. Richard Munro
Chairman of the Board: Ralph P. Davidson
Executive Vice President: Clifford J. Grum
Chairman, Executive Committee: James R. Shepley
Editorial Director: Ralph Graves
Group Vice President, Books: Joan D. Manley
Vice Chairman: Arthur Temple

TIME-LIFE BOOKS INC.

MANAGING EDITOR: Jerry Korn
Text Director: George Constable
Board of Editors: Dale M. Brown, George G. Daniels,
Thomas H. Flaherty Jr., Martin Mann, Philip W. Payne,
Gerry Schremp, Gerald Simons, Kit van Tulleken
Planning Director: Edward Brash
Art Director: Tom Suzuki
    Assistant: Arnold C. Holeywell
Director of Administration: David L. Harrison
Director of Operations: Gennaro C. Esposito
Director of Research: Carolyn L. Sackett
    Assistant: Phyllis K. Wise
Director of Photography: Dolores A. Littles

CHAIRMAN: John D. McSweeney
President: Carl G. Jaeger
Executive Vice Presidents: John Steven Maxwell,
David J. Walsh
Vice Presidents: George Artandi, Stephen L. Bair,
Peter G. Barnes, Nicholas Benton, John L. Canova,
Beatrice T. Dobie, Carol Flaumenhaft, James L. Mercer,
Herbert Sorkin, Paul R. Stewart

THE EPIC OF FLIGHT

Editor: Jim Hicks
Designer: Donald S. Komai
Chief Researcher: W. Mark Hamilton

Editorial Staff for The RAF at War
Picture Editor: Robin Richman
Text Editors: Russell B. Adams Jr., Lee Hassig, Gus Hedberg
Writers: Glenn Martin McNatt, William Worsley
Researchers: Marguerite Johnson, Maria Zacharias
(principals), Patricia A. Cassidy, Nancy Cromwell Scott
Assistant Designer: Van W. Carney
Copy Coordinators: Elizabeth Graham, Anthony K. Pordes
Art Assistant: Anne K. DuVivier
Picture Coordinators: Rebecca C. Christoffersen,
Betsy Donahue
Editorial Assistant: Stafford Levon Battle

Editorial Operations
Production Director: Feliciano Madrid
    Assistants: Peter A. Inchauteguiz, Karen A. Meyerson
Copy Processing: Gordon E. Buck
Quality Control Director: Robert L. Young
    Assistant: James J. Cox
    Associates: Daniel J. McSweeney, Michael G. Wight
Art Coordinator: Anne B. Landry
Copy Room Director: Susan B. Galloway
    Assistants: Celia Beattie, Ricki Tarlow

Correspondents: Elisabeth Kraemer (Bonn); Margot
Hapgood, Dorothy Bacon, Lesley Coleman (London); Susan
Jonas, Lucy T. Voulgaris (New York); Maria Vincenza Aloisi,
Josephine du Brusle (Paris); Ann Natanson (Rome). The
editors also wish to thank: Robert Gilmore (Auckland); Helga
Kohl (Bonn); Peter Hawthorne (Johannesburg); Judy
Aspinall, Karin B. Pearce (London); John Dunn (Melbourne);
Marcia Gauger (New Delhi); Carolyn T. Chubet, Miriam
Hsia, Christina Lieberman (New York); M. T. Hirschkoff
(Paris); Mimi Murphy (Rome).

THE AUTHOR

Ralph Barker served in the RAF during World
War II as a wireless operator and air gunner.
While in the service he wrote two books
about the War—Down in the Drink and The
Ship Busters. Since his retirement from the
RAF in 1961 he has written 20 other non-
fiction books and some 200 feature articles
for the London Sunday Express.

THE CONSULTANTS for The RAF at War

Robin Higham, Professor of History at Kan-
sas State University, served in the RAF from
1943 to 1947. He is the editor of two scholar-
ly journals, Military Affairs and Aerospace
Historian, and has written several books on
the history of British military aviation.

John McIntosh Bruce, who received a master
of arts degree from the University of Edin-
burgh, is the author of many authoritative
books and articles on historic aircraft. A former RAF pilot, he is Keeper of Aircraft and
Research Studies at the RAF Museum, Hendon, London, and a fellow of the Royal Aero-
nautical Society.

THE CONSULTANTS for The Epic of Flight

Charles Harvard Gibbs-Smith was Research
Fellow at the Science Museum, London, and
a Keeper-Emeritus of the Victoria and Albert
Museum, London. He wrote or edited some
20 books and numerous articles on aeronau-
tical history. In 1978 he was the first Lind-
bergh Professor of Aerospace History at the
National Air and Space Museum, Smithsoni-
an Institution, Washington.

Dr. Hidemasa Kimura, honorary professor at
Nippon University, Tokyo, is the author of
numerous books on the history of aviation
and is a widely known authority on aeronau-
tical engineering and aircraft design. One
plane that he designed established a world
distance record in 1938.

For information about any Time-Life book, please write:
Reader Information
Time-Life Books
541 North Fairbanks Court
Chicago, Illinois 60611

Library of Congress Cataloguing in Publication Data
Barker, Ralph, 1917-
    The RAF at war.
    (The Epic of flight)
    Bibliography: p.
    Includes index.
    1. World War, 1939-1945—Aerial operations, British.
2. Great Britain. Royal Air Force—History—World War,
1939-1945. I. Time-Life Books. II. Title. III. Series:
Epic of flight.
D786.B2597   940.54'4941   81-5297
ISBN 0-8094-3293-5
ISBN 0-8094-3292-7 (lib. bdg.)
ISBN 0-8094-3291-9 (retail ed.)

CONTENTS

A rush for manpower to meet the threat of war

In a furious debate in the House of Commons in July 1934, Winston Churchill alarmed his colleagues with the news that Germany's Adolf Hitler was secretly building an air arm that within two more years would be able to overwhelm Britain's Royal Air Force—unless the RAF expanded at once. Over the protests of members who denied there was any real threat of war, Parliament voted to keep the RAF at parity with the growing German air force. This would mean building up the RAF's manpower and replacing its aged fleet of biplanes with faster monoplanes.

The task would not be easy. Operating on a shoestring since World War I, the RAF had been reduced to a nucleus of only 30,000 men and was the world's most glamorous, exclusive and impoverished gentlemen's flying club. In the words of its first Chief of the Air Staff, Sir Hugh Trenchard, the RAF had become "a very good cottage on the foundations of a castle." The RAF College at Cranwell trained pilots at a leisurely rate, usually fewer than 60 a year. To get a permanent RAF commission without passing through Cranwell, even students from Oxford or Cambridge were generally required to graduate with high honors—and all candidates had to train in RAF-sponsored flying clubs while at the university. But as war approached, the RAF opened its doors wider every year during the late 1930s, granting thousands of temporary Short Service commissions to adventure-seeking volunteers. To bolster its full-time forces, the RAF established several reserve organizations of civilian part-timers and ex-RAF officers.

When Britain went to war in 1939, its air force had quadrupled to a strength of 118,000 regulars. However, it had not maintained parity with Germany. The Luftwaffe, by now an aerial armada with more than 500,000 men, outnumbered the RAF several times over in both pilots and planes. A year later, German bombers would demolish the parliamentary debating chamber where Churchill had implored his nation to make greater haste in rearming. And the question of Britain's survival would be debated in the sky by the new pilots of the RAF. Said one eagerly: "Visions of great air battles floated before us."

Standing in ranks outside a London recruiting office in 1939, young Britons receive final instructions before departing for RAF training.

With the aid of a half-dismantled Siskin fighter, an RAF sergeant lectures Cambridge undergraduates on aircraft design at their flying club. The students got practical flying experience at a nearby RAF airfield.

A flight instructor at the Cranwell RAF College uses a model with movable controls to show cadets how to bank an airplane. The blackboard behind them records the flying hours of each trainee.

Learning to fly the RAF way, members of the Oxford University Air Squadron meet at an RAF airfield for their annual two weeks of training.

Practicing with a Lewis machine gun, a standard weapon in British combat aircraft, an RAF recruit sets his sights on a static paper target.

Getting the feel of the bombardier's berth, a trainee lies prone in the nose window of an Oxford Airspeed trainer. For a mission, a bombsight would be fitted in the window.

Five weeks prior to the outbreak of the War, cadets of the RAF College at Cranwell pass in review before the Chief of the Imperial General Staff during graduation ceremonies at which they were given their commissions as pilot officers.

Getting help with parachutes and flying harnesses, pilots of No. 19 Squadron, the first RAF unit to fly the Spitfire fighter, prepare to take off on a demonstration flight in May 1939. Within a year, Spitfires would be flying in combat against the Luftwaffe.

The first taste of combat: a bitter surprise

On a crisp November morning in 1939, three British pilots stationed at Vassincourt, a primitive grass airfield 50 miles southeast of Rheims, raced for their Hawker Hurricane cockpits. Seconds later, their planes bumped and juddered across the undulating field, then folded their wheels in a prayer-like gesture before climbing away in pursuit of a German Luftwaffe reconnaissance plane that had been reported deep inside French territory.

When the British pilots reached 20,000 feet in a sky left crystalline by a torrential rain, they had a panoramic view of northern France from the Ardennes Forest to the winding Marne River. Leading the Hurricanes was Flying Officer Cyril D. Palmer, one of 15 young Royal Air Force pilots, all inexperienced in combat, who had flown to France with No. 1 Squadron on September 8, 1939. Britain and France had declared war on Germany five days earlier in response to the invasion of Poland.

Soon Palmer spotted the enemy plane, a Dornier 17 bomber. He was able to identify it from the characteristic outline—pencil-like fuselage and bulbous nose—familiar to him from the aircraft-recognition books that he had studied in his spare moments during squadron training. The German bomber, its pilot apparently aware of the British fighters, was racing for the frontier, but the Hurricanes were faster by nearly 70 miles per hour and soon drew within range. Streaking up from behind, the British aircraft opened fire. Against the combined fire of three eight-gun fighters, the Dornier had no chance of escaping unscathed. After a hail of machine-gun fire from the Hurricanes, one of the Dornier's engines started belching smoke and flame, and the plane began to lose altitude.

Palmer watched as the German gunner and navigator tumbled from the smoking fuselage and pulled the rip cords of their parachutes. Diving in on the bomber for the *coup de grâce,* he pressed down on the Hurricane's firing button. Nothing happened; he had run out of ammunition. Fortunately, the Dornier appeared to be doomed anyway. Closing in from behind, Palmer could see the German pilot slumped over the controls. Anxious to satisfy himself that the pilot was indeed dead and the plane certain to crash, Palmer eased back on

During the early days of the War, British pilots (left) confer with their French allies at an airfield in France. In the background is a Fairey Battle bomber, outdated even at this stage of the fighting.

his throttle and brought his Hurricane alongside the crippled bomber.

Inside the glass nose of the Dornier, its pilot, Corporal Arno Franken-berger, was playing possum. His plane had been severely damaged, but he himself had not been hit. Now, with a sudden jerk on the throttle, he brought his engines almost to a halt. The Dornier slowed immediately, leaving Palmer's Hurricane out in front. Frankenberger then swung his plane in directly behind Palmer and went into action. Momentarily abandoning the flying controls, he climbed into the seat vacated by his navigator, locked an MG 15 machine gun into position and fired a long burst into the rear of the Hurricane.

At the clatter of bullets ripping into his fuselage, Palmer ducked and pushed his stick abruptly forward, causing his Hurricane to nose down sharply and drop beneath the German's line of fire. A single bullet had penetrated the locker behind him, skimmed past his head and smashed his windshield. The burst of fire had also stopped his engine.

Palmer's quick reaction saved his life—but he would never have been in danger had he been experienced enough not to let his curiosity overcome caution. Trailing a white cloud of glycol vapor from a punc-tured cooling system, he coasted safely to a nearby field. His landing gear had been damaged, so he brought his plane down on its belly. Frankenberger, in no position to tangle with the other two Hurricanes, which all the while were firing at him, landed the Dornier not far from Palmer and was immediately taken prisoner by a squad of Frenchmen. The German pilot's adventures, however, were not over.

After spending the night in a French jail, Frankenberger—despite the vehement protests of the French officials—was released into the custody of the British pilots for the following evening. Taken to the upstairs room in a small inn near Vassincourt that served as the British officers' mess, the bewildered German prisoner was cordially wel-comed, ushered to a seat by the fire and given a frothy tankard of beer. During the course of the evening, Frankenberger dined on the best food available in the small village, proudly displayed snapshots of his wife and baby, and presented his captors with a signed photograph of him-self. Well after midnight, when he, Palmer and the others had drunk a toast to the fraternity of all pilots, the Britons and their captive part-ed in a merry glow—they to stumble back to their quarters, he to be carted off to imprisonment.

Such camaraderie, with its echoes of World War I chivalry, accorded oddly with the idea of total war. But to the RAF pilots, the War as they would come to know it—the ordeal of Dunkirk, the fight to save Lon-don, the desperate defense of Malta and the dogged struggle in the air over Europe—had not yet begun. Later, the survivors would look back at the initial, gentlemanly confrontations that began in September of 1939 and call them, in the language of the country where much of the early action took place, *La drôle de guerre*—the Phony War.

War had been declared, yet neither side had mounted an offensive. The large, well-drilled German Luftwaffe seemed to be waiting for its enemies to make the first move, but Britain and France struck a defensive posture, marshaling forces along France's northeastern frontier. Britain had flown 10 Fairey Battle light-bomber squadrons of Bomber Command to bases in France to form the nucleus of the Advanced Air Striking Force (AASF). Two Hurricane fighter squadrons, Nos. 1 and 73, followed. Another unit, called the Air Component and intended to provide tactical and reconnaissance support for British ground forces, arrived soon afterward. It consisted of twin-engined Blenheims and single-engined high-wing Lysanders to be used for reconnaissance, backed up by Hurricanes and Gladiators, the latter being durable but lamentably outdated biplane fighters. But the RAF dared no aggressive action beyond attacking enemy reconnaissance flights that crossed the border and launching a handful of bombing missions against German warships.

There was, of course, nothing phony about the hundreds of lives and scores of planes lost in maintaining this frustrating stance. But the knowledge that both sides were stopping short of using their full military might added a sense of unreality to the early days of the conflict.

Yet valuable lessons were learned by the RAF during this period; in fact, one came from Palmer's aerial tangle with Frankenberger. The Hurricane had an armored fuel tank and a bulletproof windshield, but nothing to protect the pilot from the rear—an omission that had nearly cost Palmer his life. Palmer's squadron commander, Patrick J. H. "Bull" Halahan, was quick to request rear armor plating for his Hurricanes, but his request was refused on the ground that the plating would disturb the plane's center of gravity. Not to be deterred, Halahan fitted back armor in one aircraft himself and then had one of his pilots persuade the experts with a breathtaking display of aerobatics. Thereafter, back armor became standard in both the Hurricane and the Spitfire. However, not all the lessons learned during the eight months of the Phony War that preceded the German blitzkrieg through the Low Countries and France would be as painless as this.

Although the RAF lacked combat experience, it was nonetheless temperamentally suited to fighting. Ever since it had been established as a separate service in April 1918 by the amalgamation of the Army's Royal Flying Corps and the Royal Naval Air Service, the Royal Air Force had been fighting for its life. Both the War Office and the Admiralty argued that air power must be subordinate to operations on land and sea—and that a separate service for fliers was quite unnecessary. On several occasions, Parliamentary supporters of the RAF had to fight off proposals to divide it up between the Army and the Navy.

A parallel threat emerged with the British War Cabinet's adoption, in 1919, of the notorious "Ten Year Rule," which was based on the presumption that the British Empire would not have to fight a major war within the next 10 years. Renewed annually until 1932 as the cornerstone of British defense policy, the Ten Year Rule thwarted the

Shielding his eyes from the sun's glare, Lord Trenchard—accompanied by a young squadron leader—watches an RAF display in the spring of 1939, ten years after his resignation as Chief of the Air Staff. A staunch advocate of a strong British air arm, Trenchard was widely regarded as the father of the Royal Air Force.

development of stronger armed services, particularly of the young—and still largely experimental—Royal Air Force.

Fortunately for the RAF and, as it turned out, for Britain, a man of rare foresight led the fight against this tendency to neglect the development of air power. Sir Hugh Trenchard, Chief of the Air Staff, nicknamed Boom because of his stentorian voice, was a visionary whose single-minded advocacy of strategic air power had all the strengths and weaknesses of an obsession. At the heart of his philosophy was the unshakable conviction that attack was the best defense, and that the strategic bomber, which would hit military and industrial targets, was the key to victory. Trenchard argued—and eventually convinced Parliament—that the Air Force would be best able to perform this kind of mission as an independent service, separate from land and sea forces.

Shackled by the economic stringency of the post-World War I years, Trenchard nonetheless pressed ahead to build a sound basis for his fledgling force. He set up the RAF College at Cranwell for the training of officers, and at Halton, an apprenticeship program for ground crewmen. His Auxiliary Air Force, a band of weekend fliers recruited from young men of substance who could afford the costs involved, boosted the number of squadrons at scant government expense. Then, in 1934, came Winston Churchill's assertion in the House of Commons that a secret air force existed in Germany.

Suspicion turned to certainty in 1936 when Hitler sent troops and two squadrons of fighters into the Rhineland, reclaiming control of that German area, which had been demilitarized by the Versailles Treaty. The British responded with a new emphasis on the design and production of modern aircraft and a vast program of airfield construction that eventually was to turn the country into an island aircraft carrier. In 1936 a new volunteer reserve began recruiting and training some 800 pilots a year to staff the three major RAF operational commands: Bomber, Fighter and Coastal.

By 1939, the RAF had established a frontline force of dependable aircraft. Bomber Command relied on Wellingtons and Whitleys, classified as heavy bombers; Hampdens and Blenheims, medium bombers; and the Fairey Battle, a three-man, single-engined plane that served as a light bomber. Coastal Command had twin-engined Ansons, American-built Hudson bombers and Sunderland flying boats for maritime reconnaissance. Hurricanes and a handful of newly developed Spitfires were the primary fighters. The last-moment expansion program had more than trebled the size of Britain's Air Force to some 1,500 combat-ready aircraft—but the Luftwaffe had managed to grow at an even more impressive pace and by the outbreak of the War possessed more than twice as many planes as the British.

When war finally came in September 1939, the Royal Air Force had been in existence for 21 years and regarded itself as a mature and highly professional force. As a young service, operating in a new element, it had a glamor that none of the other services could match.

The factory war

When the RAF undertook in the mid-1930s to modernize and expand its combat air fleet, British plane makers, used to a leisurely peacetime production pace, were badly underequipped for the task.

To increase manufacturing capacity, the government built a number of plants, enlisting automobile makers to manage some of them. And the aircraft industry began subcontracting work to companies ranging from furniture makers, who made jigs, wing spars and other wooden parts, to small engineering shops.

The expansion program paid off. In 1938 Britain produced 2,827 military aircraft, about half the German output. But by 1940 the British total had soared to 15,049 warplanes, nearly half again as many as the enemy produced that year.

Supermarine Spitfire fuselages await final assembly at Woolston in 1939.

On a production line at Southampton, workmen prepare Spitfires to receive their Rolls-Royce engines.

Geodetic fuselages of Vickers Wellington bombers stand on a production line at Weybridge in early 1939. The latticework construction made the planes light, yet sturdy enough to carry heavy bomb loads.

Workers swarm around rows of mass-produced Blenheim bombers in a government-owned factory near Liverpool.

As visitors watch, a traveling crane hoists a nearly completed Blenheim bomber over another plane in an earlier stage of production. The crane saved much time in bypassing assembly-line bottlenecks.

Boosted by a press that, in the early days of the War, had little else to be enthusiastic about, its pilots and crews gained a reputation for panache, which they did their best to deserve.

But the truth, which began to be revealed on September 3, 1939, when the RAF was ordered to discharge its first operational task of the War, was alarmingly different.

The task took place in a most unexpected quarter. Britain's fighters were poised on the ground in anticipation of an immediate air attack by the enemy, but its bombers were barred by political decisions from hitting land targets. Therefore the RAF was preparing, not without misgiving, to attack the Germans at sea. At 11:01 a.m., one minute after war was officially declared by the Prime Minister, a bold plan involving bomber squadrons Nos. 107 and 110, then stationed at Wattisham, 65 miles northeast of London, was set in motion.

This opening gambit was initiated by Flying Officer Andrew McPherson, a daring and persistent Scot, who set off in a Blenheim from Wyton airfield, 60 miles north of London—with a senior Navy officer as observer—to reconnoiter and photograph the North Sea bases of the German fleet. They found a concentration of warships in the Schillig Roads at Wilhelmshaven, Germany, and on a second mission the following day, saw more warships at a large naval installation near the entrance to the Kiel Canal at Brunsbüttel.

On a visit to France in late 1939 to boost British morale, England's King George VI stands beneath a Hurricane's propeller as he greets RAF officers at the Lille Seclin airfield. The tour satisfied the King that the British flier of World War II was "at least the equal of his predecessor."

On September 4, shortly after McPherson returned with his second report, 10 Blenheims led by Flight Lieutenant K. C. Doran, each carrying two 500-pound general-purpose bombs that were fitted with 11-second delay fuses for low-level attack, took off into lowering skies for Wilhelmshaven. Five Blenheims from No. 139 Squadron at Wyton took off to join the raid, but they turned back because they could not find the target in the increasingly bad weather. Doran's 10 aircraft found and entered the approaches to the Schillig Roads, where two choice targets, the small battleship *Admiral Scheer* and the cruiser *Emden,* lay at anchor.

Five bombers from Doran's No. 110 Squadron made the first attack. They had no trouble getting at the ships and scoring two direct hits on the *Admiral Scheer,* but their bombs bounced from the armor-plated decks into the water before exploding. As the planes withdrew, antiaircraft guns on the ships and ashore started firing, and one Blenheim went down. By the time the five planes from No. 107 Squadron arrived over the targets, the flak had become pulverizing. Only one bomber of that formation survived.

Meanwhile 14 Wellingtons of Nos. 9 and 149 Squadrons were heading for Brunsbüttel. Similarly hampered by the weather, they faced antiaircraft fire as ferocious as that met by the Blenheims. Two Wellingtons were lost. The rest claimed only a single hit—and that no more than a "possible."

Of the 29 aircraft that took part in these strikes, Britain's first offensive sorties of World War II, 10 failed to find their targets and seven were lost. Subsequent reconnaissance revealed that the damage to the ships had been superficial, with the exception of that inflicted by one of the felled Blenheims, which, either by chance or by a final valiant act of its doomed pilot, crashed into the bow of the *Emden.* As a bold attempt to cripple the German fleet at the outset of the War, the mission was a dismal failure.

Bomber Command did not begin scientific analysis of individual operations until June 1940, but an informal study of the raids of September 4 offered some salient pointers. Far too few British planes had been able to find their targets. Radio communications and aerial photography had been imperfect. Exposing air crews to the formidable German defenses in order to drop ineffectual bombs was wasteful and dangerously destructive of morale.

The War Cabinet decided that in the future the home-based squadrons, instead of trying to penetrate heavily fortified ports, would confine their attacks to ships at sea. But even this limited goal proved to be too ambitious. On September 29, eleven Hampden bombers detected and attacked two German destroyers in the Heligoland Bight, off Wilhelmshaven. Again, the British bombers failed to damage the German ships. The first formation of six did little more than stir up the defenses before returning to England. The second formation of five was intercepted by German fighters. Although the Hampdens, with their

narrow, tapering fuselages, afforded good visibility to pilots and were comparatively fast and maneuverable, they had no power-operated turrets and their hand-turned .303-caliber machine guns proved to be no match for the Messerschmitts' 20-millimeter cannon, which fired explosive shells. In the melee, swooping German fighters shot down the entire second formation.

The single-engined Fairey Battles proved to be even more limited. More than 2,000 of them had been built—on a design dating back to 1932. They were woefully slow and, with only two guns, had less firepower than the Hampdens. Yet Battles made up the majority of the British bombers in France at the beginning of the War. After a few disastrous clashes with the fast, well-armed single-engined Messerschmitt 109E fighters, the RAF units in France were ordered to strike with Battles only at night and to await the arrival of more of the twin-engined Bristol Blenheims before flying daylight raids.

Until it had more and better aircraft—in particular, long-range heavy bombers—the RAF could not undertake with any hope of success the strategic bombing of selected military and industrial objectives, the role for which it had sought and retained its independence. Partly for this

The British Whitley heavy bombers in this vivid painting brave a storm of flak as they drop propaganda messages. More than 65 million leaflets were showered over enemy territory in an effort designed to create dissension between the people of Germany and their Nazi leaders.

GESTAPOLEN

"Sie verwüsten ganze Länder und nennen es Frieden"

Ist das der Lebensraum, für den Ihr kämpft?

This British leaflet, which was dropped over Germany in the spring of 1940, calls attention to the Germans' oppressive occupation of Poland. "The Gestapo ravage entire countries and call it peace," said the text, then asked Germans if this was what they were fighting for.

reason, it suited the British to respect the appeal made by President Franklin D. Roosevelt to the European powers on September 1, 1939, to avoid any aerial bombardment of civilian populations. In any case, unrestricted bombing was a form of warfare in which the British preferred not to take the initiative. One reason was that they were not equipped to defend their own cities against counterstrikes. The French, whose air-defense organization was less efficient than that of the British, were even more apprehensive of German retaliation, and Bomber Command found itself condemned to lag one step behind the Luftwaffe in bombing initiative.

That fall and winter, the RAF's Bomber Command squadrons, forbidden to drop bombs on German cities, began concentrating on a new assignment: scattering propaganda leaflets over Germany. The British had started dropping leaflets the first night of the War. After a week, however, a public outcry against bombarding the Nazis with nothing more lethal than paper while Hitler devoured and digested Poland, led to the leaflet campaign being stopped. (A joke went around that bomber crews were warned to be sure to untie the bundles before dropping them lest they hurt someone below.) But two weeks later, in the naïve belief that the German people could change or influence their government, the campaign was resumed. The results were disillusioning; not only was there no noticeable reaction from the German public but the leaflet missions, like the bombing missions before them, indicated serious weaknesses in the RAF's ability to find its targets. However, the enemy air and ground defenses did little to prevent these missions, and while a few planes succumbed to bad weather while dropping leaflets, not a single aircraft was lost to German fire. As it became clear that pamphleteering had no apparent effect on the Germans, the British government accepted the fact that it would have to upgrade its offensive from leaflets to bombs.

For the previous 20 years, the British Air Staff had pinned its faith, should war come, on a strategic air offensive against selected German industrial and military targets. In the fall of 1939, development of large four-engined bombers suitable for such strikes was under way, but the planes were still 18 months or more from deployment. The four Blenheim squadrons that were in France in the fall of 1939 were barely adequate as instruments of strategic reconnaissance, but the role of long-range precision destroyers was beyond their capacity. Until the new large planes were ready, Bomber Command would have to depend on a slightly outdated yet eminently trustworthy machine, the twin-engined Vickers Wellington.

The Wellington's distinctive cigar-shaped fuselage and unusually tall single fin and rudder were to become, in the next two and a half years, familiar to everyone in Bomber Command. Its geodetic construction—thin metal members crisscrossed in a kind of basketwork pattern and covered with nothing more than a fabric skin—allowed the

Wellington to absorb amazing doses of gunfire and still remain in the air. Two power-operated turrets had two .303-caliber machine guns each. When flown in close formation in daylight, the Wellington was expected to offer a concentration of fire sufficient to repel the boldest of attackers.

Such was the belief on December 3, 1939, when—after First Lord of the Admiralty Winston Churchill had dramatically contrasted British shipping losses to U-boats and magnetic mines with England's own feeble action against the German fleet—the War Cabinet decided to strike again at the large German warships in the Heligoland and Wilhelmshaven area. Injury to the enemy's civil population was still to be avoided, however: Bombs were not to be aimed at warships in dock. A force of 24 Wellingtons, flying in tight formation unaccompanied by fighters and led by Wing Commander Richard Kellett of No. 149 Squadron, was to make the assault.

Unknown to the British, the Germans had the assistance of a primitive form of radar, called Freya, which on this occasion gave them a crucial eight minutes' warning of the approaching raid. However, a low cloud cover that frustrated the British bombers also hindered the Germans in finding the raiders. And even when the German fighters, Messerschmitt 109s and twin-engined Messerschmitt 110s, did locate the British force, they gave wide berth to the sting of the Wellington tail gunners. The latter, cramped and numb after crouching on the hard metal seats in the planes' unheated tail sections for hour after hour, manning twin machine guns that were no match for the Messerschmitts' cannon, managed to keep the German pilots at bay. All 24 bombers fought their way through and dumped their bombs but they missed the German battleships, instead sinking a minesweeper and inflicting minor damage on a shore battery.

The Wellingtons returned to base unharmed. The same degree of immunity was not enjoyed when the attempt was repeated 11 days later. On this occasion a single German fighter was shot down, but five of the 12 Wellingtons dispatched were lost, while a sixth crashed near its base. However, these losses were attributed to low-level flak—bad weather had forced the British to make a low-altitude attack—and the Air Staff remained confident that the close bomber formation, with no fighter escort, was to be the formula for success.

Thus it was that on December 18, twenty-four Wellingtons, led again by Richard Kellett, tried their luck in another raid on the Schillig Roads and Wilhelmshaven. Armed with 500-pound bombs—to be dropped from no lower than 10,000 feet, so that the planes could avoid the flak—the Wellingtons were grouped in four sections of six aircraft each. Kellett led the forward section. Shortly after leaving their airfield, two of the planes in the second section turned back, one because of engine trouble and the other because of a communications failure. But the first serious setback came 50 miles off the English coast, when the expected cloud cover began to disperse. One hundred miles out the sky became clear, with visibility up to 35 miles. No contingency plans had been made to abort the raid. Then, some 70 miles from their target, the Wellingtons tripped the German radar screen, alerting a nest of fighter-interceptors in the Wilhelmshaven area. The stage was set for Britain's costliest mission of the Phony War.

The bomber crews photographed four large warships at Wilhelmshaven, but all were in dock or in harbor, and the men obediently withheld their bombs. Although flak, mostly from shore batteries, was intense, its only effect was to force the planes in the rear sections to spread out. Then, when the flak eased, the German fighters pounced.

Approaching from abeam and above, the German pilots took full advantage of the Wellingtons' vulnerability to attacks from the flank. The forward cabin of a bomber in the leading section burst into flames and the plane crashed into the sea. Another Wellington broke apart like the pieces of a jigsaw puzzle in mid-air, and a third spiraled into the water with its port engine trailing a plume of dense black smoke. By the time the rear section flew into the trap, the Messerschmitts were stirred up to a frenzy and five of the six bombers in that group were destroyed in a blizzard of cannon fire.

The last of the Wellingtons owed its safe return to England to one of its crew members, who accidentally pulled a flap lever on his way forward to the gun turret. When the plane unexpectedly lost speed, the attacking fighters overshot. Seeing his chance, the Wellington's pilot dived his plane from 15,000 feet to just above sea level and sped for home. Behind him, Wellingtons from other sections were escaping from the fray and heading for Holland with fuel streaming from their bullet-punctured tanks.

Of the 22 planes that reached Wilhelmshaven, 10 were downed near the target, two more were so badly shot up they had to be ditched and two others were destroyed in forced landings in Britain. All of the remaining eight were damaged. After the air battle of December 18, waist guns, self-sealing fuel tanks and additional armor plating were added to the Wellingtons. But these were only marginal improvements, and any prewar illusions that Bomber Command could be effective as a daytime force were now completely destroyed.

On April 13, 1940, Bomber Command's new Commander in Chief, Air Marshal Sir Charles Portal, received a directive from the Air Staff outlining a new role for his planes. Portal was to confine the operation of his heavy bombers mainly to night action. Henceforth, Bomber Command's much-vaunted and much-delayed strategic offensive would be launched in the dark.

One bright spot in the RAF's performance thus far in the War was in France, where two Hurricane squadrons of the Advanced Air Striking Force were regularly demolishing German reconnaissance aircraft sent across the frontier. Yet even here serious problems were starting to arise. The eight-gun Hawker Hurricane could deal comfortably enough with the Dorniers, but it was no match for the Messerschmitts that sometimes accompanied them. The Luftwaffe was exacting an increasing toll from the British fighters.

Engagements during the spring of 1940 had shown that the Messerschmitt 109 was speedier than the Hurricane and dived and climbed faster. The Hurricane proved the tougher machine and the more stable gun platform, but in other respects it was outclassed; only the skill and aggression of the British pilots produced any measure of equality. The cat-and-mouse stalemate at the border was dramatically altered when at dawn on May 10, 1940, the Phony War ended and German armies began pouring into Belgium and Holland. Hitler's blitzkrieg on the Low Countries had begun.

British and French armies moved to their planned defensive positions, and the men of the RAF in France prepared to discharge their assigned duties. Eight Battle and two Blenheim squadrons of the AASF were to attack the advancing German columns at bridges and major road junctions. The Hurricanes, reinforced by a squadron from England, escorted bombers and defended airfields. Tactical and photographic reconnaissance of the section of the front manned by the British Expeditionary Force (BEF) was the responsibility of five squadrons of Lysanders, while four Blenheim squadrons searched farther afield. Six fighter squadrons, in addition to their escort duties, provided protection to British troops and bases.

This at least was the theory. But it was 11 a.m. before the French, still apprehensive of German reprisals and hoping illogically that the kid-glove war might somehow be prolonged, agreed to the bombing of the massed German columns. Finally 32 Battles, armed with delayed-action bombs and protected by an umbrella of patrolling Hurricanes, took off for a low-level attack on German columns advancing through Luxembourg. They encountered such intense flak and machine-gun fire that 13 of them were shot down and all the rest were damaged.

Early next morning the Belgian government pleaded with the RAF to bomb the bridges over the Albert Canal near Maastricht on the Dutch-Belgian border to thwart the German advance in that area. The Commander in Chief of the British Air Forces in France, Air Marshal Arthur S. Barratt—Ugly Barratt, as he was affectionately called by his men—responded at once and had one of his Blenheim squadrons at Condé-Vraux, No. 114, refueled and loaded with bombs for a 6 a.m. takeoff. Just as the crews were climbing into the Blenheims, nine Dornier 17s appeared above the top of a line of trees and fanned out over the airfield, making directly for the parked bombers. Six of the Blenheims were destroyed and the rest were badly damaged. In a stroke, half of Barratt's medium-bomber force was eliminated. Throughout the rest of the day Dorniers and Heinkels continued to pummel the French and British airfields.

Meanwhile the bridges over the Albert Canal near Maastricht remained intact. When the Belgian Air Force tried to destroy them, six of

Braving the bitter French winter of 1939-1940, members of an RAF ground crew remove a tarpaulin from a snow-covered Fairey Battle. Wrote one RAF pilot: "Snow and ice were everywhere, and it was impossible to keep warm, indoors or out."

Crewmen inspect an idle bomber, one of many French-based RAF planes grounded by wet engines or flooded fields during the 1940 spring thaw.

the nine planes sent on the mission were shot down before they could reach the targets, and the three that got through failed to do any damage. Twelve Britain-based Blenheims from Bomber Command's No. 2 Group made a final attempt to bomb the bridges before nightfall, but they were jumped by German fighters on the approach and lost a third of their number. No one hit the bridges.

Although German forces were known to be massing in the Ardennes, the dense forest region of northeastern France and southern Belgium, the French generals still believed that the penetration at Maastricht would be the main enemy thrust, and that night Barratt received two urgent messages from London stressing the importance of destroying the Albert Canal bridges.

But he was also under great pressure to harass the German troops from the air, and at dawn the next day he sent his only remaining Blenheim bomber squadron, No. 139, to attack an armored column advancing toward Tongres, Belgium. Of the nine Blenheims dispatched, seven failed to return; Barratt's entire medium-bomber force had been almost annihilated.

With his Blenheims gone, Barratt had virtually no bombers available for an attack on the Albert Canal bridges. In desperation, he played his last card. A squadron of Fairey Battles—the obsolescent and undergunned light bombers—would be sent in, escorted by a protective

A member of an RAF photographic unit delivers an air reconnaissance camera to the crew of a Bristol Blenheim Mark IV. After the lumbering bombers proved easy prey for German flak and fighters, they were replaced on reconnaissance flights by swift Spitfires equipped with extra fuel tanks.

umbrella of Hurricanes. The mission would be for volunteers only.

Early the next morning the crews of No. 12 Squadron had the mission explained to them. Two bridges, a metal one at Veldwezelt and a concrete one at Vroenhoven, were to be destroyed at all costs. Three planes were to attack each bridge.

Each Battle would carry its normal crew of three: pilot, navigator and gunner. Most of the gunners were ground crewmen who had volunteered for flying duty.

The two section leaders, Norman Thomas and Donald "Judy" Garland, both in their early twenties, chose their own methods of attack. "I'm going in at low level," Garland told Thomas as they strode across the airfield to where their planes were concealed at the edge of the surrounding woods. "You'll get shot to pieces," replied Thomas. "It's dive-bombing for me."

One of the three planes in Thomas' section suffered a hydraulic failure and was unable to take off. The other two leveled out at 7,000 feet and set course through scattered clouds for the concrete bridge at Vroenhoven. They were followed five minutes later by Garland and his section bound for Veldwezelt. The fighters—including Hurricanes of No. 1 Squadron, located at another airfield and led by Bull Halahan— were making straight for the Maastricht area.

The distance to the bridges was 120 miles, and it took the Battles an

An intelligence officer peering into a stereoscope that made three-dimensional images analyzes pictures taken by British reconnaissance fliers. Sidney Cotton, leader of the reconnaissance unit, remarked that such analysis "required the patience of Job and the skill of a good darner of socks."

hour to get there. Thomas arrived first over the target and attracted an intense barrage. Suddenly, the flak stopped, but Thomas knew why. Off his starboard wing a Messerschmitt was bearing in on the two British planes. The other Battle, flown by Pilot Officer T. D. H. Davy, would have to fight off the intruder alone. Thomas fixed his eyes on the bridge below and, pressing his stick forward, began his dive, gently at first, and then steepening until the plane was almost vertical. The old Battle shrieked and shuddered as its altimeter unwound and the gunner and navigator struggled to hold their positions. At 3,000 feet, Thomas began releasing the 250-pounders in his bomb rack. Using the spinner on the propeller to align the plane with the bridge, he continued cutting loose his bombs until, 400 feet from the ground, he heaved back on the stick. The plane, groaning from the stress and lurching violently in the shock waves of the last bomb, leveled out and then began to climb. But a holocaust of flak forced Thomas to roll his nose groundward, leveling off at an altitude of some 20 feet for a fast, treetop-skimming getaway.

Flak had hit the starboard wing and the navigator was plugging a ruptured fuel line with his finger. Suddenly, as the fields and hedges sped by beneath them, the engine coughed and went dead. Thomas dropped the plane neatly onto its belly in a field of grass and skidded to a stop. Thomas, his navigator and his gunner, all unhurt, were immediately taken prisoner.

Above him, Davy, who had broken loose from the German fighter and emptied his bomb racks in the vicinity of the bridge, went streaking toward home leaving a trail of dense black smoke behind him. His port fuel tank had been badly damaged by the German fighter. Close to the border, he ordered his crew to bail out. One landed in France and remained a free man, and the other, who jumped before the plane crossed the border, spent five years in prison camp. Davy flew on by himself, eventually bringing his Battle down in a field a few miles from his base. It was later learned that neither Davy nor Thomas had succeeded in destroying the bridge.

All three Battles in Garland's section reached the bridge at Veldwezelt. As they approached the target, Garland radioed the other two pilots, Flying Officer I. A. McIntosh, an Australian, and Sergeant Fred Marland. "We're going in low-level as planned," he ordered, as he led the section down to an altitude of 50 feet. Bull Halahan and his Hurricanes had meanwhile stormed into the attack, but they were heavily outnumbered. As Garland's section bored in, six Hurricanes and three Messerschmitts lay smoldering beside the canal.

McIntosh's machine was hit and burst into flames. The Australian was forced to turn away from the target, jettison his bombs and belly-land in a field. From the ditch in which he and his air crew sought shelter they watched as one of the other two Battles, now hopelessly crippled, staggered away from the target with flames pouring from the canopy. The watchers winced as the stricken Battle pulled up vertically, then

Pilots of No. 87 Squadron, Royal Air Force, scramble to their Hurricane fighters at an airfield in France in March of 1940.

dropped its nose down and plunged to earth, where the aircraft exploded in a blinding fireball.

Whose plane exploded was never learned with certainty, although it was believed to be Marland's. The one remaining Battle—probably Garland's—was hit on the final approach. It seems likely that the pilot, remembering the exhortation at briefing that "the bridges must be destroyed at all costs," purposefully dived his plane into the span hoping that the impact of the crash coupled with the explosion of his bombs would complete his mission. Whether by accident or design, the plane struck the bridge, and when the smoke cleared the span was severed, the shattered truss hanging in mid-air. Judging that the Battle that hit the bridge was Garland's, the British government posthumously awarded him and his navigator, Sergeant Thomas Gray, the Victoria Cross, Britain's highest honor for valor; theirs were the first air Victoria Crosses of the War.

On May 14, when the Allied generals finally realized that the main German thrust was aimed not through Maastricht but to the south through the Ardennes and Sedan, the French implored the British to join them in a concerted attack. Barratt had 71 bombers left, and almost all of them were old Battles. In a desperate play, he sent all 71 planes into combat; 40 were lost.

On May 19 the possibility of evacuating the entire British Expeditionary Force from the Continent was tentatively discussed in Whitehall. Two days later the Germans reached the Channel coast, separating the bulk of the French Army south of the Somme and Aisne Rivers from the British and Belgian Armies to the north. Now there was no choice. The British Expeditionary Force had to retire to the port of Dunkirk and somehow escape across the Channel to safety. Otherwise it would be annihilated, leaving Britain virtually without an army.

Coveting the prestige of victory, Hermann Göring, Commander in Chief of the Luftwaffe, urged Hitler to entrust the final destruction of the BEF in France to his bombers, contending that they could do the job most quickly and economically. The blitzkrieg had shown the Luftwaffe at the peak of its resilience and efficiency; a free rein to discharge this task would be the final accolade.

Göring, the opportunist, had played his hand nicely: Hitler agreed to his proposal. The pace of the German advance had been bewildering, for the Germans as well as the Allies, and on May 24 General Gerd von Rundstedt's tanks, hot on the heels of the retreating BEF, were commanded to halt 20 miles from the English Channel. By the time this order was rescinded, a strong Allied rear guard had been formed to hold the German armor off the beaches.

"The Luftwaffe is to wipe out the British on the beaches!" gloated Göring. But the Luftwaffe had been hotly engaged by the RAF and the French during the German thrust, and the units involved were now at 30 per cent of their former strength. Moreover, a new factor had been added to the British side of the equation. The first Spitfire squadrons were ready to fight. "I pointed out to Göring," wrote Field Marshal Albert Kesselring, commanding Luftflotte 2, one of the three German air fleets on this front, "that the modern Spitfires had recently appeared, making air operations difficult and costly." But Göring chose to ignore this warning.

The German pilots themselves did not underestimate the Spitfires. One of the first encounters between a Spitfire and a Messerschmitt occurred on May 22, four days before the evacuation began, when Alan Deere, a young New Zealander in No. 54 Squadron, ran out of ammunition with his Spitfire poised close behind an Me 109. Deere decided to hold his position if he could; if he broke away the German would guess his trouble. He found that he could turn inside the German as the Messerschmitt corkscrewed and switchbacked, could hold him on the straight and level, and could stay with him in the climb. Only when going into the dive was the Me 109 superior, its direct-injection carburetor giving it the edge as the Spitfire's engine, drained of fuel at that angle, cut out. Deere was then left behind, but by half-rolling his plane so that fuel from the carburetor was thrown into the engine instead of out, and by turning inside the 109 as it came out of the dive, he caught up. At last, as their fuel ran low, both pilots broke off and headed for home.

On May 26 the evacuation of the British troops from Dunkirk began in earnest. The RAF's defensive cover worked well at first. Formations of Spitfires and Hurricanes at squadron strength took off every 50 minutes from bases in southeastern England and headed across the Channel. "Enemy fighter activity very strong," one German recorded in an army corps diary, "our own fighter protection completely lacking. Use of Luftwaffe against sea transport ineffective."

On May 27, however, with the defending French troops forced back to a perimeter five miles from Dunkirk, stepped-up German air attacks on the town and harbor threatened to overwhelm the evacuation. Fighter Command's patrols were quickly becoming outnumbered. Fortunately, a cloud of black smoke rising from burning oil tanks hung over the town and hampered the German pilots. Still, the Luftwaffe would not be shaken off, and the troops being evacuated suffered cruelly under successive attacks.

Early the following morning the Chief of the Air Staff, Air Chief Marshal Sir Cyril Newall, addressed his three operational commands. "Today is likely to be the most critical day ever experienced by the British Army. I am confident that all ranks will appreciate that it is the duty of the RAF to make their greatest effort today to assist their comrades of both the Army and the Navy." Bomber and Coastal Commands, as well as Fighter Command, were deeply engaged. Blenheims attacked German troops closing in on the perimeter by day, and Hampdens and Wellingtons, supported by the few Battles remaining in France, attacked German lines of communication at night.

Air Vice Marshal Keith Park, the 48-year-old New Zealander who

Defended by RAF fighter planes, British soldiers in this contemporary painting flee the beaches of Dunkirk under heavy German shelling.

directed the fighter cover for the evacuation, flew over Dunkirk himself in a Hurricane. His firsthand experience of the situation convinced him that the number of fighters in each patrol must be boosted from two squadrons (24 aircraft) in the air at a time to four squadrons. But, with only 18 squadrons at his command, Park realized that this plan would mean lengthening the 50-minute intervals between patrols. His pilots were already dangerously overtaxed, and their allotment of time on the ground to rest and eat could not possibly be shaved down any further. Park's only hope was to obtain a few more fighters from Fighter Command's home-defense squadrons but, to Park's astonishment, his request was refused: The Air Staff, at the behest of Air Chief Marshal Sir Hugh Dowding, head of Fighter Command, was unbending in limiting the allotment of fighters for the evacuation.

Both the Hurricane and the Spitfire were intended to be defensive aircraft and consequently were built with relatively small fuel tanks. They could fight for only a few minutes over Dunkirk before they had to return to England to refuel. Moreover, they were greatly outnumbered over the French beaches even when Park, on May 29, doubled the patrol strength to four squadrons at a time, although he had been allotted no additional aircraft. And the longer intervals between patrols made necessary by this change allowed two of the five major attacks by the Luftwaffe that day to go completely unopposed.

Incidents like this gave birth to an angry lament that was to poison British interservice relations for many months: "Where was the RAF?" Pounded mercilessly from the air as well as from the shore, the soldiers of the British Expeditionary Force cursed the RAF as the corpses of their comrades piled up on the beach and bobbed face down in the gentle breakers off the Pas-de-Calais.

A parade of warships, private yachts, barges, ferries, fishing boats and even a Yangtze River gunboat fought through the bombs to Dunkirk and then streamed back to England, each vessel jammed to the gunwales with Tommies. The Stukas found these ragtag rescuers easy targets and, starting their dives from a safe position behind the German lines, screamed down out of the cloudy skies to bomb and strafe the overloaded vessels as they struggled out to sea.

On June 5, when 338,226 Allied troops had been carried in ignominious retreat across the Channel and thousands more left dead on the French coast, the question of what more the RAF should have done to clear the skies of Dunkirk turned into a shrill condemnation of the entire service. Pilots and ground crewmen were insulted on the streets of London, and soldiers and sailors alike seethed with resentment about what they regarded as the puny efforts of the RAF to protect them. Who was to blame? The accusing fingers all pointed at one man: Sir Hugh Dowding. But the starchy, strong-willed Commander in Chief of Fighter Command, whose concern for Britain's need for fighters after Dunkirk had led him to restrict the number of planes committed during the evacuation, seemed sublimely unmoved. ~~

The planes that fought the opening rounds

The best RAF fighters and bombers of the early War years were the result of farsighted planning. It took about four years to get a new type of warplane into service after the Air Ministry issued specifications for it; most of the aircraft presented here were conceived years earlier but came into full production just in time for the War.

To meet Fighter Command's need for a fast monoplane, planners started work on the Hawker Hurricane in 1933. A year later, development began on the nimble Supermarine Spitfire fighter. The Wellington and Whitley bombers were ordered in 1934 to replace Bomber Command's aging biplanes. The Bristol Blenheim was an exception; it was hastily adapted from a civilian transport design and rushed into production in 1935.

Some of the planes on these pages are later models rather than the first of their type. Roman numerals indicate the model number, and the date is the year that model entered service. Adjacent planes are in scale to each other.

SUPERMARINE SPITFIRE I (1938)
Though it closely resembled the Hurricane, the Spitfire was 35 mph faster and far more maneuverable. This one is painted in the camouflage it wore in the Battle of Britain, when it was flown by the famed No. 610 Squadron, based at Biggin Hill, Kent.

HAWKER HURRICANE I (1937)
The first British interceptor to be armed with eight wing-mounted machine guns, the Hurricane was the RAF's workhorse fighter at the outbreak of war. This one flew with No. 85 Squadron in France until the unit's bases were overrun by the enemy in 1940.

BRISTOL BLENHEIM IV (1939)
When the prototype of this bomber appeared in 1935 it was faster than many fighters, but by the outbreak of war the Blenheim was no match for German interceptors. This plane, wearing desert camouflage, served in North Africa.

BRISTOL BEAUFORT I (1939)
With experience gained from the Blenheim, the Bristol company designed this tough twin-engined torpedo bomber for the RAF's Coastal Command. It carried one 1,605-pound torpedo in a semienclosed fuselage bay and had four machine guns.

VICKERS WELLINGTON III (1941)
The Wellington's geodetic frame, visible in the side window, helped the bomber survive penetration by bullets and flak. Air crews called it the Wimpy because the portly craft reminded them of the hamburger-loving cartoon character. Its underside is painted black to provide night camouflage.

ARMSTRONG WHITWORTH WHITLEY V (1940)
The Whitley's ungainly appearance led pilots to dub it "the flying barn door," but it was dependable and the first British bomber with power-operated gun turrets. The letters DY stand for No. 102 Squadron, and the R identifies the specific plane.

"NEVER WAS SO MUCH OWED BY SO MANY TO SO FEW"

THE PRIME MINISTER

2
The battle for survival

When the telephone rang at Number 10 Downing Street at 7:30 in the morning on May 15, 1940—11 days before the evacuation of the British Expeditionary Force from Dunkirk began—Winston Churchill was still asleep. Because the call, from Paris, was extremely urgent, it was put through to the Prime Minister's bedside. Churchill heard the voice of French Premier Paul Reynaud exclaim, "We have been defeated."

It was true. With one sudden rush of tanks and motorized infantry, Hitler had put the French Army to rout and now bade fair to take the whole country in a matter of weeks. Churchill had been in office only five days—he had succeeded Neville Chamberlain as Prime Minister on May 10—but he had few doubts about Hitler's next target. Great Britain was the only power that stood between the German dictator and complete mastery of Western Europe.

Two hours later, Churchill met with the chiefs of staff of the Army, the Navy and the Royal Air Force to discuss Reynaud's request for 10 RAF fighter squadrons to be sent to the aid of France. Air Chief Marshal Sir Hugh Dowding, Commander in Chief of Fighter Command, had asked to attend the meeting in order to state his case before the new Prime Minister. A tall, lean 58-year-old widower, Dowding was an aloof— some said lonely—man whose forthrightness often made others uncomfortable. His superiors also found him awkward to deal with because of his seniority, which exceeded even that of the Chief of the Air Staff, Sir Cyril Newall. Dowding considered France lost and was reluctant to send any more of his fighter squadrons across the Channel. Like Churchill, he knew that Hitler would soon turn on Great Britain, and he was afraid that Britain would be unable to defend herself if more RAF planes were lost in an ultimately doomed attempt to save France.

Even four months earlier, when the RAF had still had 51 fighter squadrons to defend Britain, the Air Staff had considered that total inadequate. Now Dowding had only 36 squadrons left in Britain, yet he feared that unless he intervened the War Cabinet, which was to meet later that morning, would vote to send some of these across the Channel. Churchill, who had a tenderness almost beyond reason for France, was prepared to make a costly stand on the Continent.

As the meeting progressed, Dowding's worst suspicions were confirmed. Churchill wanted to go to France's aid; to do this he suggested sending the 10 squadrons Reynaud had asked for. The chiefs of staff,

In this wartime poster, five RAF sergeants— pilots and gunners—stand beneath the famous quotation from Winston Churchill's August 20, 1940, speech before the House of Commons. The British government published the poster as an expression of the nation's gratitude for the RAF's performance during the Battle of Britain.

who should have realized the dangers involved, were just at the point of agreeing with the plan when Dowding rose from his chair and walked to where the Prime Minister sat. On the table in front of Churchill he placed a graph that showed how the number of British fighters under his command had declined as they continued to confront the Germans in France. The graph lines dropped precipitously.

If Fighter Command continued to defend France, Dowding said quietly, there would be no fighters left to protect Britain from the German attack that would surely come. The implications of both the graph and Dowding's reasoning were clear to Churchill. He had hoped to send at least 10 fighter squadrons to help France; he now agreed to send none. Later that day, after Dowding had gone, Churchill changed his mind and ordered four squadrons of Hurricanes to France. But then he decided that a piecemeal defense was worse than none and, conceding finally to Dowding's argument, withdrew the Hurricanes after only three days. Churchill, always the bulldog, hated to retreat, and Dowding ever afterward was convinced that the Prime Minister bore him a grudge for forcing this concession from him.

The next day Dowding sent a letter to the Air Ministry reiterating the points he had made at the meeting, and adding:

"Once a decision has been reached as to the limits on which the Air Council and the Cabinet are prepared to stake the existence of the country, it should be made clear to the Allied Commanders on the Continent that not a single aeroplane from Fighter Command beyond the limit will be sent across the Channel no matter how desperate the situation may become."

Then, less than two weeks later, Fighter Command was called upon once again to commit itself outside Britain. Thousands of British troops, fleeing the victorious Germans, were trapped on the beaches at Dunkirk. While they were being evacuated they desperately needed air cover. For Dowding, the choices were agonizing. Fighter Command would, of course, try to clear the skies over Dunkirk, but the risks were enormous. "All such fighting," said Dowding, "militates against the maintenance of a force adequate to protect this country in the event of our having to carry on a war single-handed against a power possessed of all the resources of Europe." In a letter to the Air Staff he made his point more bluntly. "I earnestly beg," he wrote, "that my commitments may be limited as far as possible unless it is the intention of the Government to surrender the country in the event of a decisive defeat in France."

During the evacuation of Dunkirk, Fighter Command flew 2,739 sorties—a sortie is a single flight by one plane—across the Channel. The pilots flew to the point of exhaustion and then kept on flying. Yet they received little credit from the soldiers below. The RAF's battles with German planes were seldom visible to the troops because of the heavy cloud cover and thick smoke that hung over the French coast. Also, the British fighters tried to intercept the Germans as far as possible from the

The austere visage of Air Chief Marshal Sir Hugh Dowding manifests the granite determination that characterized his leadership of the Royal Air Force's Fighter Command through the Battle of Britain.

Air Vice Marshal Keith Park, here in flight suit and inflatable life jacket, commanded No. 11 Fighter Group, which defended London and southeastern England in 1940.

The forthright demeanor of No. 12 Group leader Air Vice Marshal Trafford Leigh-Mallory contrasts with the reputation for intrigue he acquired among other officers.

battlefield; a great portion of the air fighting took place miles away from Dunkirk. In the end, 106 RAF fighters were lost and 75 pilots were killed or taken prisoner, but these figures could not be released to the public at the time. When both soldiers and civilians expressed anger that the RAF had not done more to help the evacuation, Winston Churchill came to the defense of the airmen.

Addressing Parliament on June 4, the last day of the evacuation, he said, "We must be very careful not to assign to this deliverance the attributes of a victory. Wars are not won by evacuations. But there was a victory inside this deliverance which should be noted. It was gained by the Air Force. This was a great trial of strength between the British and German air forces. Can you conceive a greater objective for the Germans in the air than to make evacuation from these beaches impossible? They tried hard and they were beaten back. I will pay my tribute to these young airmen." And then he struck a prophetic note: "The great French Army was very largely, for the time being, cast back and disturbed by the onrush of a few thousands of armored vehicles. May it not also be that the cause of civilization itself will be defended by the skill and devotion of a few thousand airmen?"

Dowding's reaction to the fall of France, recorded by Lord Halifax, who visited him later that month at Fighter Command headquarters, was terse. "Thank God," he said, looking out his window in the general direction of the English Channel, "we're now alone."

For years before the War began, Hugh Dowding had been preparing for the Battle of Britain. He was certain that someday the RAF and the Luftwaffe would meet in British skies, and he devoted most of his effort as head of Fighter Command to getting ready for that day. But on the eve of the confrontation for which he had planned so assiduously, there was a chance that Dowding would not direct Britain's fighter force in the battle. In fact, at the time of Dunkirk he was in danger of being retired in a matter of weeks.

Dowding had once been heir apparent to the title of Chief of the Air Staff. However, in 1937 he had been passed over in favor of Sir Cyril Newall. Then in 1939 Dowding had been due to retire, but his appointment as Commander in Chief of Fighter Command was extended until the end of March 1940. He was then left in suspense about his future, right up to the penultimate day of that month, when Newall asked him to continue until July 14.

The truth was that Dowding had long been an embarrassment to the Air Staff. As Fighter Command's stubborn leader he had pushed relentlessly to build up his force for Britain's defense, even at the expense of Bomber Command and the Trenchard doctrine of the offensive favored by the Air Staff. But Fighter Command was essentially his creation, and to replace him at this critical stage would not be easy. Thus on July 5, nine days before he was due to retire, Dowding was asked to remain in his post until October. The defense of England was in his hands, and his

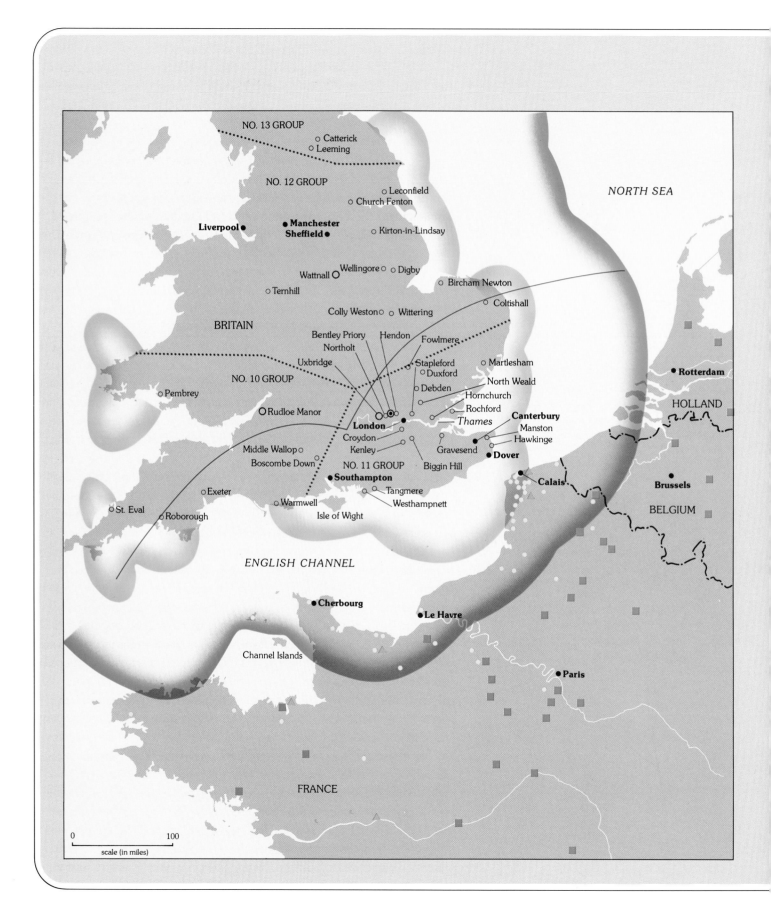

NO. 13 GROUP
○ Catterick
○ Leeming

NO. 12 GROUP
○ Leconfield
○ Church Fenton

● **Liverpool** ● **Manchester** ○ Kirton-in-Lindsay
Sheffield ●

Wattnall ○ Wellingore ○ Digby
○ Ternhill ○ Bircham Newton

BRITAIN Colly Weston ○ ○ Wittering ○ Coltishall

Bentley Priory Hendon Fowlmere
Northolt
Uxbridge Stapleford ○ Martlesham
NO. 10 GROUP ○ Duxford
○ Pembrey North Weald
○ Debden
○ Rudloe Manor Hornchurch
Rochford **Canterbury**
London ● *Thames* Manston
Croydon Hawkinge
Kenley Gravesend ● **Dover**
Middle Wallop ○ **NO. 11 GROUP**
Boscombe Down Biggin Hill Calais
● **Southampton**
○ Exeter Tangmere
○ Warmwell Westhampnett
○ St. Eval Isle of Wight
○ Roborough

NORTH SEA

● **Rotterdam**

HOLLAND

Brussels

BELGIUM

ENGLISH CHANNEL

● **Cherbourg** ● **Le Havre**

Channel Islands

● **Paris**

FRANCE

0 ————— 100
scale (in miles)

The forces arrayed

"The English Air Force must be eliminated to such an extent that it will be incapable of putting up any substantial opposition to the invading troops," said Adolf Hitler on July 16, 1940. This map shows the German and British deployments on August 13, 1940, the day the Luftwaffe launched the assault designed to carry out Hitler's decree.

The Germans had divided three air fleets—almost 3,500 airplanes in all, including bombers, dive bombers and fighters—among 79 bases in Belgium, Holland, France, Norway and Denmark. Me 109s were concentrated at coastal bases in France to bring as much of England as possible within range (red line).

The RAF had only about 900 serviceable fighters to fend off the Germans. These were spread among 53 bases (40 are marked here, the rest being north of the area shown). The country was divided into four defensive zones, each of which was the responsibility of a Fighter Command group. The heaviest concentration of bases was in No. 11 Group's zone, directly across the Channel from the German fields in France. The total air-defense effort was coordinated from Fighter Command's headquarters at Bentley Priory, near London.

To maximize the effectiveness of its meager fleet of combat planes, the RAF deployed a combination of long-range, high-level and short-range, low-level radar systems (green shaded bands).

ROYAL AIR FORCE
- ■ HIGH-LEVEL RADAR RANGE
- ▪ LOW-LEVEL RADAR RANGE
- o FIGHTER COMMAND STATION
- ◉ FIGHTER COMMAND HEADQUARTERS
- O FIGHTER COMMAND GROUP HEADQUARTERS

LUFTWAFFE
- — ME 109 RANGE
- ∙ FIGHTER BASES
- ▲ DIVE-BOMBER BASES
- ■ LONG-RANGE BOMBER BASES

defense plan, which involved an elaborate system of airfields, communication networks and early-warning devices, was to remain intact.

Dowding had split his command into three groups (opposite). No. 11 Group was to defend London and the south, by far the most vulnerable area because of its proximity to the Luftwaffe bases in France. No. 12 Group was to defend the eastern counties and the industrial Midlands. No. 13 was to defend Scotland and northeast England. Congestion in the southeast soon obliged Dowding to create a fourth group, No. 10, to cover the southwest, but the largest, most important groups remained Nos. 11 and 12. Each group was divided into sectors, and the sector airfields were the basic operating units in Dowding's defense line.

Dowding's plan called for cooperation between groups once the fighting started, and for this he relied on his group commanders. The group most likely to need assistance was No. 11, commanded by Air Vice Marshal Keith Park. He had been Dowding's Senior Air Staff Officer, and his appointment to the crucial command of No. 11 Group, one of the most sought-after jobs in Fighter Command, had been a controversial one. When command of the group had fallen vacant in the spring of 1940, the likely replacement seemed to be Air Vice Marshal Trafford Leigh-Mallory, who had commanded No. 12 Group since 1937. But Dowding appointed Park to No. 11 Group and left Leigh-Mallory where he was.

Blunt and incisive, Leigh-Mallory was a dedicated, ambitious career officer. He had the reputation of being an able commander but a restless subordinate. On one occasion, during a stormy visit to Dowding's headquarters at Bentley Priory, he vowed to Park that someday he would get Dowding sacked. When Park was chosen to lead No. 11 Group, Leigh-Mallory made no secret of his envy. Thus Dowding faced the War with an avowed and determined foe in his own ranks.

He was also short of aircraft, but that problem was being solved. Churchill had named as Minister of Aircraft Production a dynamic Canadian who had become a wealthy and powerful London newspaper proprietor, William Maxwell Aitken, Lord Beaverbrook. The 61-year-old Beaverbrook was reluctant, but Churchill persisted. He told Beaverbrook that the output of fighters must take precedence over all other military manufacture until the expected German assault was repulsed. With this fiat in hand, Beaverbrook single-mindedly swept all obstacles aside. Poaching personnel and commandeering property, not caring whom he offended, he so galvanized the aircraft industry that Dowding's frontline fighter strength rose from 331 at the end of the Dunkirk evacuation to more than 600 a month later.

One of Fighter Command's greatest assets was a system of air-raid warning and ground-to-air control unparalleled at that time anywhere in the world (page 53). The system depended primarily on secret and relatively recent British advances in the application of radar. The principle of radar—that the position of an object can be discerned by transmitting powerful radio waves toward it and reading the radio echoes that bounce back—had been discovered in the late 19th Century. Practical development had been slow, but by 1936 the British—then well ahead of the Germans or any other nation in the practical application of this technology—had begun building a chain of coastal radar stations that could detect enemy aircraft while they were still over the Continent or the Channel.

In the RAF's air-raid-warning system, ground observers would visually track the attacking planes once they were over Britain. Radar and observer reports would be funneled to a central information clearinghouse at Bentley Priory, called the filter room, where the enemy aircraft's positions were plotted on a large map table and disseminated to the operations rooms of the various fighter group headquarters and sector stations. In the weeks before the battle the early-warning network was tested incessantly, with British aircraft taking the roles of enemy planes, until the system neared perfection.

The RAF's formula for intercepting a raid, as evolved during these tests, was made up of several fixed elements and a number of imponderables. The first inkling of an impending attack would probably come when radar scans caught the German bombers joining their fighter escort over the Pas-de-Calais, some 25 minutes' flying time from the nearest No. 11 Group sector stations. The pilots of a well-practiced RAF fighter squadron could scramble—rush to their planes and get them airborne—in two or three minutes after the first warning. The British aircraft then needed about 15 minutes—slightly less for Spitfires, slightly more for Hurricanes—to climb to an altitude of 20,000 feet. Thus, if all went well for the RAF, its fliers had a few minutes' margin of safety in their race to intercept the intruders.

The attackers, it was true, could strike where they chose—but the defenders, using their wall of radar, would rarely be taken completely by surprise. This advantage was not yet appreciated by Hitler. On July 16, after spending nearly two months vainly trying to get the British to agree to immediate peace, he summoned his service chiefs and ordered them to prepare for the imminent invasion of the British Isles.

Hitler's War Directive No. 16 and subsequent orders issued by the Luftwaffe's commander, Hermann Göring, were equally unequivocal: The German air force was to employ all the means in its power to destroy Fighter Command. Three Luftwaffe divisions called Luftflotten, or air fleets—Luftflotte 2 in northwestern France and the Low Countries, Luftflotte 3 in northeastern and southern France and Luftflotte 5 in Scandinavia—would take turns attacking Dowding's ground organization and British fighter factories. Once air superiority was achieved, the air war was to be continued against ports and harbors. Through all this the Luftwaffe must remain battleworthy for the invasion. Hitler reserved for himself the right to order ''terror raids as reprisals.''

The date Hitler issued his war directive, July 16, is considered by many the beginning of the confrontation that would be known to the world as the Battle of Britain. But for almost a month after July

Fighter Command's secret eyes

The network of radar stations and visual observers that tracked enemy planes for the RAF during the Battle of Britain was the most efficient air-raid early-warning system in the world—and, despite the involvement of thousands of people, one of the world's best-kept secrets.

Twenty-one long-range radar stations on England's south and east coasts could detect enemy bombers 140 miles away at altitudes up to 30,000 feet. Most intruders who slipped in under this screen were spotted by short-range, low-level radar stations. And after the attackers crossed the English coast, they were tracked with binoculars and other sighting instruments by trained civilian observers who were posted throughout the countryside.

Reports were fed to an information clearinghouse, known as the filter room, in Fighter Command's headquarters at Bentley Priory, near London. There, people called plotters kept track of enemy and RAF positions by moving colored markers on a giant map table. Others watching from a balcony above the map immediately telephoned new developments to group and sector headquarters, where similar map tables were kept abreast of the action and radio-equipped controllers directed RAF fighter aircraft accordingly.

"The British fighter was guided all the way from takeoff to his attack on the German formations," Luftwaffe General Adolf Galland wrote later. "For us this was a surprise and a very bitter one."

The 185-foot tower of a low-level radar station stands guard near Felixstowe, on England's east coast.

Inside a radar receiving hut, an operator searches her screen for telltale blips warning of the approach of Luftwaffe aircraft.

Civilian volunteers scan the sky above England from their observation post. The woman's telescope-like apparatus is a sighting device that was used to measure the altitude and bearing of enemy aircraft.

In No. 11 Fighter Group's headquarters at Uxbridge, near London, controllers in a glassed-in balcony watch as plotters with magnetic rakes manipulate markers showing the positions of hostile and friendly aircraft.

Bentley Priory in Middlesex, built as a country estate in 1788, served as Fighter Command headquarters during World War II.

16, German air attacks were mainly restricted to British shipping in the Channel. In the second week of August, Göring judged the time was right for stronger measures. He believed that, given fine weather, fighter opposition in southeast England could be quelled in four days and air mastery extended throughout Great Britain in four weeks. August 13 was to be the first day of this bold venture and he named it *Adler Tag*—Eagle Day.

On August 12, in preparation for Adler Tag, German bombers struck at British harbors, radar stations and coastal airfields. When dawn came on August 13, the Luftwaffe bomber airfields in northern France were clouded over and bathed in a drizzling rain. Nonetheless, 74 Dorniers of Luftflotte 2 took off shortly after 5:00 a.m., missing Göring's orders to postpone the raids until the afternoon, and continued on toward England without fighter cover. Protected by clouds, they bombed Eastchurch airfield on the Isle of Sheppey in the Thames estuary. They were under the impression that they were striking a fighter base. But German intelligence had made an error: Eastchurch belonged in fact to Coastal Command—and it was operational again within 10 hours.

Taking off in pairs, sleek British Spitfires race to engage attacking German bombers over England during the summer of 1940.

Because of the bad weather and the confusion over the postponed start, fewer planes struck Britain that day than Göring had intended—but their 1,485 sorties were sufficient to provide a dramatic beginning for the offensive designed to eradicate Fighter Command. All over southern England the men of Dowding's fighter squadrons got their first taste of the frantic rush to battle that would characterize their lives for weeks to come. In the southwest, the pilots of No. 609 Squadron from Warmwell scrambled on orders from No. 10 Group and saw faraway telltale specks in the sky that soon were identified as 30 Ju 87 Stukas—dive bombers—approaching with a powerful fighter escort. The Luftwaffe pilots were using the same wavelength as the British, and presently the No. 609 Squadron fliers began to hear German voices in their earphones shouting *"Achtung—Spitfeuer!"*

A handful of Spitfires had begun to attack the German fighters, but the bulk of No. 609 Squadron hung high in the sky at about 20,000 feet, where the blinding afternoon sun made them invisible to the incoming German formation below. As the enemy dive bombers swept on toward their target, Squadron Leader H. S. Darley led his fighters in a wide arcing descent that brought them in unnoticed directly

behind the Germans. At the last moment, Darley shouted "Tallyho" into his radio, and the attack began. When Pilot Officer David M. Crook spied five Me 109s swooping in beneath him, he broke formation and dived on the hindmost. "I gave him a terrific blast of fire at very close range. He burst into flames and spun down many thousands of feet into the clouds below."

Below them, on one of the cliffs above Portland, Winston Churchill, accompanied by Major General Bernard Montgomery, then commander of the British Army's V Corps, broke off a survey of coastal defenses to marvel at the spectacle. During the fight, five of the Stukas and three of the escorting Me 109s plunged into the sea. To the northeast, two squadrons of Ju 88s were heading for the Fighter Command sector station at Middle Wallop, but they lost their way and bombed a grass airfield near Andover by mistake. By the end of the day, the Germans claimed 70 Spitfires and Hurricanes destroyed, although in fact Dowding lost only 13 fighters in the air and one on the ground. Of the 64 victories claimed by the RAF in its 700 sorties, 46 were later confirmed. So ended the long-awaited Eagle Day.

Göring suspected that Dowding's strong resistance in the south of England had been achieved by denuding the Midlands and the north of fighter protection, and he decided that the way to expose this British gamble was with a combined thrust from all three Luftflotten. The weather had prevented him from opening his assault on Britain in this fashion, but on August 15 conditions improved in the afternoon and the combined attack was mounted.

It was to begin with a feint across the North Sea by Heinkel 115 seaplanes from Luftflotte 5 in Norway. These aircraft were to draw off British fighters based in Scotland while 72 of Luftflotte 5's He 111 bombers made the real strike farther south, on airfields near Newcastle on England's northeast coast. The German attempt at deception went wrong when the main bomber force and its escorting Me 110s inadvertently followed closely behind the seaplanes, dramatically reinforcing the signals received by British radar and leaving no doubt that a major attack was coming. The raiding force was put to rout, thanks largely to bold anticipatory measures by the No. 13 Group commander, Air Vice Marshal Richard E. Saul, who called up fighters from throughout his zone and vectored them onto the German bombers.

Air Vice Marshal Leigh-Mallory, Saul's opposite number in No. 12 Group, was less bold in meeting another Luftflotte 5 attack, this one aimed at airfields in Yorkshire, some 75 miles south of Newcastle. A formation of twin-engined Ju 88 bombers managed to break through the two squadrons of fighters Leigh-Mallory sent up in its path, and 10 Whitleys were destroyed on the ground at Driffield, Yorkshire. Nevertheless Saul's strike was sufficient to put Luftflotte 5 out of the battle.

In the south the raids continued all day. A savage attack on an aircraft factory at Rochester, east of London, did great damage, but the factory was building bombers rather than fighters. Other Luftwaffe bombers missed their primary targets, the vital RAF sector airfields of Biggin Hill and Kenley, and hit instead the less important fields at Croydon and West Malling.

By the end of the day, the Luftwaffe had flown almost 2,000 sorties against Fighter Command's 974. In terms of British aircraft lost—34 were destroyed—the day was Göring's. But previous RAF success in shooting down enemy bombers had forced the Germans to field stronger fighter escorts; bombers made up only a third of that day's raiding force, and similar ratios were maintained in subsequent raids. The Me 109s that were intended to range freely to gorge their appetites on Dowding's fighters would now find themselves totally absorbed in close escort work, a major triumph for Dowding and Park. And, as on Eagle Day, some of the most destructive raids did little to weaken Fighter Command, the major obstacle to a German invasion.

Göring's next move was sensible enough. Henceforth, he ordered, "operations are to be directed exclusively against the enemy air force," and he railed against the prodigal waste of effort on targets that had "absolutely no connection with our strategic aim." A further conclusion in his summary showed less perception. "It is doubtful whether there is any point in continuing attacks on radar sites, in view of the fact that not one of those attacked has so far been put out of action." This analysis was translated into Luftwaffe policy. Göring, it appeared, was still confident that he could bludgeon the RAF into submission with the sheer numbers of his fighters.

The next day, August 16, the Luftwaffe mounted 1,715 sorties. Many of the more spectacular raids again had minimal impact on Fighter Command. Of eight airfields that were bombed, only three housed fighter squadrons.

During these attacks, fierce clashes occurred between German and British fighters all along the southern coast of England. There were numerous acts of great courage on both sides—including one that resulted in the award of the only Victoria Cross given to a fighter pilot during the War. Flight Commander James Nicolson, a 23-year-old Londoner wounded in a clash off Southampton, was struggling to get out of his blazing Hurricane when an Me 110 drifted into his line of fire. Ignoring the flames in his cockpit, Nicolson dropped back into his bucket seat and pressed the firing button. The German pilot tried desperately to escape Nicolson's attack, but the Englishman held on. The fire was already peeling off the flesh of his left hand, in which he held the throttle lever, but Nicolson stayed in the cockpit until he got off a final burst and saw the Messerschmitt go down. Only then did he bail out.

During these first few days of intense fighting, the British rapidly took the measure of their opponents and adjusted their defenses accordingly. The Me 109 fighters that escorted Göring's bombers were formidably fast planes, and whenever possible, Fighter Command's swift new Spitfires were sent up against them. The slower Hurricanes were then assigned to strike at the bombers. From the RAF's point of view, this was the ideal matchup. Yet, with Hurricane squadrons outnumbering Spitfire squadrons nearly two to one, there were frequent exceptions. On these occasions, the Hurricane pilots would try to capitalize on the major advantage their planes had over the enemy's: a much smaller turning radius.

Such was the case on August 18 when the men of Hurricane Squadron No. 85 from Debden were beset by a swarm of Me 109s while making a routine attack on some Heinkel bombers. Peter Townsend, the British squadron leader, had learned a maxim for dealing with 109s—"Never climb, never dive; just turn"—and immediately applied it when out of the corner of his eye he caught sight of a Messerschmitt diving on him. When he pulled his plane into a hard turn, the attacking aircraft slid harmlessly by, disappearing below him. Seconds later, it reared up in front of him and began a wide left-hand turn, apparently intending to come around and attack him from behind.

"It was a fatal move," Townsend later recalled. He, too, swung his plane into a left-hand turn—a much tighter turn than the German could possibly make—and fell into position for a flank attack. He fired and the Messerschmitt spun over in the air and burst into flames. Townsend's victory was not a fluke; minutes later he bagged another Me 109 when its pilot tried to outmaneuver him with a similar sweeping turn.

At Biggin Hill that day, two Hurricane squadrons met nine Dornier 17s that swept in at about 100 feet to bomb the airfield. Two of the Dorniers were shot down, two more crashed and three limped back to France badly damaged. Another hedgehopping force of Dorniers had better luck raiding Kenley airfield. Evading British fighters, the bombers demolished 10 hangars, six Hurricanes and two Blenheims and damaged many more planes. Most communications were cut and the sector operations room had to be moved to a butcher's shop in a nearby village. But at the close of the day, the tally for the fighting in all sectors was encouraging for the British. The Luftwaffe had lost 71 planes against 39 RAF fighters downed.

After the fighting of August 18, both sides recoiled. The time had come for reappraisals. Göring's four days of intensive assault—August 13, 15, 16 and 18—had cost him 236 aircraft, yet Fighter Command was still far from beaten. Göring made his fighter force the scapegoat for his failure to win the promised ascendancy and ordered the fighter pilots to guard the German bombers even more closely in the future.

This directive was just the sort of panic reaction that Dowding and Park had hoped for. Göring, in denying his fighter pilots their favorite—and effective—free-chase role, was crippling his most devastating weapon. However, Dowding, too, had cause for alarm. The destruction of 213 Hurricanes and Spitfires in the 10 days since August 8 meant that output from the factories was no longer keeping pace with losses. At this rate Fighter Command would waste away in a few weeks.

Royal Air Force fighter planes engage German aircraft in the skies over England's Portland Harbor in this 1940 painting.

But as Göring shuffled his forces for a new attack, Dowding stuck to the line of battle he had formulated years earlier, rotating only tired and depleted squadrons and trying not to unduly weaken any of his groups. The five-day lull allowed fighter production to overtake losses, and the Civilian Repair Organisation worked 12-hour shifts to put damaged planes back in the air in response to an appeal from Beaverbrook.

At this crucial moment, the rivalry between Keith Park and Trafford Leigh-Mallory took a sinister turn. Park could rely on Air Vice Marshal Sir Christopher Quintin Brand of No. 10 Group to cooperate in the defense of No. 11 Group's airfields south and west of London when Park's own planes were in the air. But north of the Thames, Park needed help from Leigh-Mallory and No. 12 Group, and here there was friction. Although the defense of Park's fields was vital, Leigh-Mallory chafed at playing second fiddle. So did his pilots. Their relatively passive role seemed intolerable to men thirsting for action.

There was an even graver conflict—this one over tactics—between Leigh-Mallory on the one hand and Dowding and Park on the other.

At Duxford airfield in 1940, ground crews carefully load ammunition into a Spitfire's wing guns. Even a small loading error could cause the guns to jam during combat.

During the preliminary phase of the Battle of Britain, Dowding had been urged by the Air Staff to meet assaults "with superior forces and large formations"—what Leigh-Mallory called "big wings." But Dowding, with the full support of Park, had resisted, favoring smaller, more flexible formations. The chief proponent of the big-wing theory was a remarkable fighter pilot named Douglas Bader, who became an ace despite having lost both legs in a prewar crash. Bader took the big-wing idea to the extreme, advocating formations of up to five squadrons operating as a unit. In time, he convinced both his own commander, Leigh-Mallory, and the Deputy Chief of the Air Staff, Air Vice Marshal Sholto Douglas, that the big wing was the best response to the German raids.

Bader was itching to lead these wings into action. But his theory, which might have worked for No. 12 Group, geographically to the rear, struck Dowding and Park as inappropriate for No. 11 Group, which had only a few minutes' warning of attacks and could not spare the time necessary to assemble large formations in the air. Bader held that it was worth taking the extra time, even if the attacking bombers meanwhile struck their targets unhindered, so that big-wing fighter formations could shoot down greater numbers of them on their way home. His doctrine was approved by Sholto Douglas; Park and Dowding would have none of it.

The argument over the big-wing theory was far from being resolved when, on August 24, Göring renewed his assault. The raid was the first since his directive ordering his fighters to stick closer to the bombers, and the formations were so compact that only two of the 12 squadrons Park vectored toward the Germans penetrated the fighter screen. Göring's new strategy had indeed succeeded in getting more of his bombers through to their targets. But by tight-reining his Messerschmitts he had destroyed fewer British fighters and imperiled his most important objective: the gradual destruction of Fighter Command.

By midafternoon Park's squadrons were stretched thin, and he called on Leigh-Mallory to cover his airfields at Hornchurch, North Weald and Debden. No. 12 Group, seizing the chance to test the big-wing theory, responded by trying to assemble a large formation. The effort miscarried—coordinating so many planes proved extremely difficult—and only one squadron turned up to defend North Weald airfield. Unfortunately, this was No. 19 Squadron, whose Spitfires were newly equipped with an experimental cannon that was prone to jam after only seconds of use. By the time the rest of Leigh-Mallory's fighters finally arrived at Hornchurch and North Weald, fierce fires were already raging. British and German fighter losses that day were about equal—the RAF 22, the Luftwaffe 26—and Göring was satisfied.

That night, while nearly 100 enemy bombers kept up a round-the-clock offensive over southeast England, several of them lost their bearings and jettisoned their bombs on the City of London and its neighboring boroughs. These were the first bombs to fall on central

The men who kept the aircraft flying

While RAF pilots waged war over England, their ground crews sweated out the battle below, risking their lives to service and patch planes at lightning speed.

As soon as a Hurricane or Spitfire landed after a sortie, mechanics clambered aboard to inspect it for damage. While they refueled and rearmed the aircraft, a general crew of armorers, instrument experts and radio repairmen performed minor repairs. Many crews could return a plane to combat within 15 minutes. At the height of the Battle of Britain, the turnaround time in some squadrons dropped to a mere four minutes.

Many ground crewmen were wounded or killed during attacks on airfields. Although they never gained widespread public recognition as heroes, their courage was admired by the pilots whom they served. "We relied implicitly on their vigilance, skill and devotion," one fighter ace would write, "to keep our machines free of defects which could cost us our lives."

London since German Gotha bombers—twin-engined biplanes of World War I—attacked the metropolis in 1918, and the encroachment seemed to be deliberate. Churchill immediately ordered reprisal raids on Berlin. The next night 81 Wellingtons struck the German capital, bombing several sections of the city and inflicting minor damage on some residential areas.

On August 26 Park asked Leigh-Mallory to cover Debden, Hornchurch and North Weald while Park's planes from those fields flew south to intercept a German attack. Again the cannon-firing Spitfires from Duxford missed their cue, and Debden suffered extensive damage. This time, Park openly condemned Leigh-Mallory for reacting too slowly, and the bitterness between the two men exploded in a torrent of recriminations. Such squabbling could not have been more inopportune for the British. As commander in chief of the fighter force, Dowding could have directly ordered Leigh-Mallory to provide Park with the necessary support, but he chose to let his two subordinates resolve their differences themselves. As a consequence, Park's position became more and more difficult.

Over the following days Park faced an increasingly formidable enemy. Field Marshal Albert Kesselring's Luftflotte 2 was reinforced with fighters from the other Luftflotten until it had four fifths of Germany's single-engined fighter force: more than 600 planes. These were concentrated in the Pas-de-Calais area, just across the Channel from Park's territory. Göring had finally learned that his fighters had greater value as an offensive force than they did as mere escorts for bombers, and the Germans began conducting massive sweeps of Messerschmitts in hopes of luring the British Spitfires and Hurricanes into combat.

On August 29, the Germans sent over formations numbering more than 500 Me 109s. Although the Luftwaffe was made to pay for its intrusions, Park had no chance against such odds and he ordered his fighters to disengage whenever possible. Reports that British fighters had shied away from combat may have contributed to an unfounded optimism that was growing among the Luftwaffe's leaders. That same day General Kurt von Döring, the commander of Luftflotte 2's fighter organization, claimed that "unlimited fighter superiority" had been achieved, and the next day Hitler said he would announce a decision regarding the proposed invasion on September 10; if everything went well the invasion fleet would sail on September 20. Meanwhile, Kesselring mounted an all-out effort to mop up what he thought was the remnant of Fighter Command.

By midday on August 30, all of Park's 21 squadrons were airborne and 10 of them were in action in the heaviest fighting of the War so far. A lucky German hit on the main electricity grid put seven radar stations out of action and many of the German bombers arrived over England unannounced, wave after wave with scarcely a pause. This time, the covering force Park requested from Leigh-Mallory appeared, but it failed to locate a squadron of German bombers over Biggin Hill that dropped more than 30 delayed-action bombs on the field and nearby villages. And later in the day, a squadron of Ju 88s roared over Biggin Hill at low level, destroying hangars and station buildings, severing telephone lines and causing numerous casualties, including 39 dead.

Over Maidstone, Squadron Leader Tom Gleave of No. 253 Squadron, Kenley, was leading his section of three Hurricanes at 17,000 feet when suddenly the sky seemed to fill with German planes. "As far as the eye could see," he later recalled, "were rows of Me 109s riding above the haze." Turning his section against one flank of the enemy formation, Gleave bored his way into the midst of the 109s, firing at every enemy plane that crossed his path and nearly colliding with one. "Tracers passed above and below, curving downward as if I were flying in a gigantic cage of gilt wire," he said. One of his wingmen escaped from the fracas and headed off; the other, whom Gleave described as a "lion-hearted hero," charged on deeper into the formation and was never seen alive again. Gleave satisfied himself that he had destroyed at least two enemy fighters and then returned to Kenley, where he watched the rest of the battle from the ground.

For the first time Fighter Command flew more than 1,000 sorties in a single day. Many pilots flew four sorties virtually without rest. The strain was beginning to tell. Some fliers fell asleep as they ate in their mess halls. Others actually fell asleep in their cockpits the moment they completed their landings. Göring's pilots had no rotation system and were almost as tired, but they were spared the protracted tensions of dawn-to-dusk vigilance.

On August 31 Luftflotte 2 flew 1,300 fighter sorties. Concentrating on Park's sector airfields, four separate bomber formations swept across the Channel, their shield of outriding fighters almost impenetrable. Flying Officer James Coward, a pilot in the unlucky No. 19 Squadron, was living with his wife in a farmhouse near Duxford at the time. A young man of superb physique and supreme self-confidence, he had been badly shaken by the repeated failure of his cannon-firing Spitfire. "Pray for me today," he told his wife as he left home before dawn. Three hours later, in the midst of aerial battle, his guns jammed and enemy fire ripped through his plane. Wounded, he pulled himself out of the cockpit of his plunging aircraft. As he floated beneath his billowing parachute, Coward saw his foot twisting and flopping at the end of a thin string of ligament connecting it to the rest of his leg. Blood poured from the severed arteries. Pulling a radio cord from his helmet, he stemmed the flow by rigging a tourniquet around his thigh before hitting the ground within a mile of his home. It proved impossible to save his leg, but citing the example of the legless Bader he talked his way back to operational flying.

In a two-pronged assault, one wave of Heinkels made for Hornchurch and the other for Biggin Hill, where the dead from the day before still lay unburied. The vital sector operations room was hit, and the hastily repaired telephone lines were severed a second time.

Two of the station's three squadrons had to be moved elsewhere.

Hornchurch, 25 miles northeast of Biggin Hill, was the scene of a frantic scramble as the pilots of 11 Spitfires of No. 54 Squadron raced to take off before the German bombers arrived. The last section of three aircraft was only inches off the ground when the bombs began to fall. One of the pilots was New Zealander Al Deere, already a seasoned combat veteran. A bomb exploded just under his plane during his takeoff. The Spitfire was tossed onto its back and skidded across the field. Deere crawled out of the wreckage with his face badly lacerated, but he was back in action the next day.

By nightfall Fighter Command had lost 39 planes in combat; an additional 10 Spitfires had been destroyed on the ground. The attrition was so great that Beaverbrook's organization was unable to keep pace with the losses. Six out of seven of Park's sector airfields were badly damaged, and one of his squadrons had been almost annihilated. More serious was the fact that more than one quarter of Dowding's pilots had been killed or wounded. Desperate for reinforcements, he had agreed in the last week of August to use some 200 foreign pilots, mostly Polish and Czech, despite the language problems involved. They were men whose fanatical hatred of the enemy made them fearsome adversaries, and they did outstandingly well from the start. They flew in squadrons composed mainly of their fellow countrymen, and, in the end, of the 10 highest-scoring aces of the Battle of Britain, one was Polish and another Czech. Dowding was grateful for the foreign fliers; as September began, Fighter Command needed all the help it could get.

Morning after morning in the first few days of September the Women's Auxiliary Air Force radar operators watched the enemy planes assembling over Calais and heading across the Channel, to be followed by waves of German bombers throughout the day. On September 1, Biggin Hill suffered its sixth raid in three days, and two WAAF telephone operators who stayed at their posts as the bombs fell were awarded the Military Medal for devotion to duty. The RAF defense was valiant but British losses were occurring at roughly the same rate as German losses, and Göring had more planes.

The rolling hills and idyllic villages of England's southern counties by now were dotted with the wreckage of this ferocious fighting. Both German and British planes fell from the sky daily, crashing into fields, trees and cottages. RAF pilots resorted to parachutes only when they were absolutely sure their planes could not be landed, choosing when they could to bring down salvageable wrecks at the risk of their own lives. Pilot Officer Tony Woods-Scawen smashed out his front teeth trying to land his crippled Hurricane on the Isle of Wight after a dogfight. He made his way to Southampton by ferry, by which time it was too late to get back to his squadron base at Tangmere that night. He drowned his sorrows in a Southampton hotel with such company as he could find and telephoned the squadron adjutant the next morning. "If you want me to go on fighting," Woods-Scawen said, "you'd better send some-one down here to pay my bill." Scores of other pilots were less lucky and many a tiny village suddenly acquired an instant hero in a young RAF pilot who lost his life fighting in the air overhead. Tony Woods-Scawen did not remain lucky for long, in fact. He and his older brother Patrick were both killed before the Battle of Britain ended, the only brothers to die in the battle.

Between August 24 and September 6 Dowding lost 466 fighters and received only 269 new and repaired machines in replacement, a deficit of almost 200. His sector airfields, although not quite knocked out, were in Park's words "pretty groggy." Worst of all, in the last fortnight 103 fighter pilots had been killed or listed as missing, and another 128 had been wounded. For all the pounding it had taken, however, Fighter Command was still capable of organized resistance.

Nonetheless, the Germans seemed intent on proceeding with the invasion plans. Across the Channel, Belgian, Dutch and French sea-ports were filling with barges. Bombers had been transferred from Scandinavia to France. Britain's Combined Intelligence Committee concluded that an invasion was imminent and that moon and tide would be favorable between September 8 and 10. In fact, the Germans had chosen September 24 as the most favorable day; but even that was little more than two weeks away.

On September 2, using Wellington raids on Berlin as a pretext, Hitler had ordered attacks on the populations and defenses of Britain's big cities, particularly London. On September 4, in a speech at the Berlin Sportpalast, he promised that the Luftwaffe would raze Britain's towns and cities one by one. A directive from Supreme Headquarters ordered an attack on London on September 7.

On the appointed day Göring, posturing on the cliffs at Cap Gris-Nez in France with Kesselring, focused his binoculars on the white cliffs of Dover directly across the Channel and exulted as more than 900 Luftwaffe planes—about 600 of them fighters—headed for London. For once British intelligence was caught napping; Dowding was given no inkling of the German onslaught. Park's dispositions were intended to cope with attacks on sector airfields and aircraft factories, and to compound his unreadiness he had been called to a conference that day at Dowding's headquarters.

By the time the true nature of the German attack was realized it was too late to stop the main force of bombers from reaching the outskirts of London virtually unopposed. The few pilots who made interceptions were confronted by an awesome sight as the dark galaxy swept forward across the sky. "There several miles away was a black line in the sky," wrote Flying Officer George Barclay, "35 Hun bombers in close for-mation—and I gradually began to distinguish about 70 to 100 other little dots—fighters."

Barclay's squadron turned to attack. "We went in at the bombers.

Followed by his faithful dog Binder, Pilot Officer Percy Prune—a creation of RAF cartoonist Bill Hooper—ambles away from a Spitfire he has wrecked. Known as "the legendary fool of the RAF," Prune filled the pages of the training manual Tee Emm, demonstrating errors to avoid.

P/o PRUNE SAYS - "A GOOD LANDING IS ONE YOU CAN WALK AWAY FROM"

But before one could take stock of the situation the Messerschmitts were on me. I turned quickly to see if there was anything on my tail and at the same moment two 109s went past beneath my nose. I turned, diving on one and gave him a burst—nothing happened. Presumably I had missed him, but the noise of my eight guns gave me great confidence. I gave the second Me 109 a burst. A sudden flash of brilliant flame, a cloud of smoke, and a vast piece flew off it, and down he went."

Barclay fired his last bullets into a big twin-engined Dornier; as he raced for his home field, he saw one of the Dornier's engines spewing black smoke, but he never learned whether he had brought the German bomber down.

London was hit savagely that day. In less than 90 minutes, and in broad daylight, more than 300 tons of bombs fell on the city, mostly on the East End and the dock areas. The RAF lost 38 planes and 20 pilots killed or wounded, against German losses of 29 planes. Fighter Command had been overwhelmed.

There was no respite that night as Göring sent another 318 bombers over the burning city. For Londoners, the count the next morning was doleful: 448 citizens killed and more than 1,000 injured. Göring's glee was unrestrained. He made a triumphant radio broadcast and telephoned his wife to tell her that "London is in flames." Dowding, although horrified by the damage done to London, was, as ever, mainly concerned about his valuable fighters. In fact, he had always expected Hitler to succumb to the temptation to strike at London instead of more important targets such as airfields and factories. In fact, he had counted on it. "The nearness of London to German airfields," he had forecast soon after Dunkirk, "will lose them the war." Park, airborne in his personal Hurricane over the burning city, was thinking along the same lines. By taking advantage of the short period of respite provided by this change in German strategy, Fighter Command could pull itself together and spring back like a tiger.

The bombing went on through a second night, killing another 412 Londoners and blocking every rail route to the south. But Dowding was rapidly resuscitating his defenses. On the following day, when Kesselring's planes returned over Britain, Park was ready for them. Park's tactical mastery of a small but disciplined force was never more brilliantly displayed, and the German stretch to reach London gave him time to operate his squadrons in pairs, against Luftwaffe fighters that were at the limit of their range. Outnumbered by the RAF, many of the German fighters were forced to abandon the German bombers altogether, forming moving circles to defend themselves. Many bomber crews, radioing distress signals back to France, jettisoned their bombs and fled—only to find their retreat cut off by more No. 11 Group squadrons. The RAF destroyed 28 German aircraft while losing only 19 fighters, and London and its population emerged almost unscathed. The result was a disturbing setback for the Luftwaffe; Hitler, impressed by the British resistance, delayed his decision to invade.

Bad weather then slackened the pace of the daylight raids, but the night bombing continued. Although Hitler still shrank from authorizing intentional attacks on residential areas, the list of targets was extended to London's railroad stations and public utility works. Between September 8 and September 14, some 2,000 Londoners were killed and more than 10,000 were injured; among the buildings damaged was Buckingham Palace.

Meanwhile, Bomber Command, still concerned over the invasion threat, destroyed many of the invasion barges that were waiting at the continental Channel ports.

Göring, still operating on the assumption that Dowding's force had been reduced to only a handful of airplanes, fixed his final bid for supremacy for Sunday, September 15. Every available bomber and fighter was to be hurled into two titanic assaults. British intelligence officials not only knew of the raid; they knew when it was coming and that it would come in two waves. With Nos. 10 and 12 Groups in support, Park was able to order his entire force to immediate readiness and to warn his pilots that they would have to land and refuel in great haste in order to catch the second wave of attackers.

Winston Churchill, accompanied by his wife, Clementine, arrived at Park's underground operations room at Uxbridge, west of London,

While a local constable protects the plane from souvenir hunters, a British Army major examines a downed Heinkel 111 in August of 1940. The German bomber had been bested by a Hurricane of No. 253 Squadron over southeastern England.

soon after the first radar reports came in. They watched as the colored symbols representing British and German planes were manipulated on the big map by WAAF plotters. The counters representing the vanguard of 100 Dornier bombers and 400 fighters were advanced inches toward the English coast.

When, at 11:30 a.m., the planes crossed the coast, Park had 11 squadrons in the air. To the RAF pilots, the approaching airborne armada looked at first like a giant staircase rolling forward. But soon the German fighter pilots were unable to shield the bombers as the British smashed through the Messerschmitt formations. The German fighters broke away to engage their attackers.

At that point Park threw another 10 squadrons at the bombers. Unprotected by their escorts, the big planes took a terrible mauling. Douglas Bader, who was supposed to be defending Park's northernmost airfields and the northern perimeter of London, could not resist abandoning that assignment and flying south with his Duxford wing to join in the fight. He added a five-squadron punch to the rout.

Knowing the pattern the raid would take, Park threw off the restraint he had imposed on himself all summer and sent up his last four squadrons. Noticing the absence of ready squadrons on the board at Uxbridge, Churchill inquired, "What other reserves have we?" Park replied laconically, "There are none."

As the bombers that had managed to elude Park's net straggled back to France, Göring and Kesselring ordered the second wave to take off. This wave included a sweep of free-chase fighters that was intended to flush the sky of Spitfires and Hurricanes and let the bombers through.

It was a clear afternoon, and for nearly an hour Londoners craned their necks skyward, watching the growing tracery of contrails as Royal Air Force fighter planes swooped and dived in mortal struggle with the German invaders. Any British doubts about the courage and commitment of Fighter Command that may still have lingered from Dunkirk were forever erased.

When the second wave of German bombers reached the East End of London, Bader and the Duxford wing pounced. Then eight more squadrons from Nos. 11 and 12 Groups surged in head on. The German fighter pilots, their fuel-warning lights blinking insistently, could not linger, and the demoralized German bomber crews jettisoned their bombs and prepared to fight their way out. For them it was the worst day of the battle. They lost 40 bombers.

Sunset found Britain in a state of euphoria: 185 German planes had been reported shot down. This was a gross exaggeration—it was three times the true figure—but the actual German losses were enough to convince the Luftwaffe that RAF Fighter Command, far from being crippled, was stronger than ever. For the bomber crews the shock of meeting some 300 fighters in the space of 20 minutes, after all the bland assurances of German numerical superiority, had been appalling.

Smoke and flames billow from the London docks after a September 7, 1940, Luftwaffe raid during which 300 tons of bombs fell on the city.

Göring still talked glibly of the annihilation of the RAF within four or five days, but other German officers knew better. On September 16 the German Naval Staff concluded that the RAF was by no means defeated and that, with autumn nearing, the calm seas necessary for a landing in barges could no longer be expected. On September 17 Hitler postponed the invasion until further notice.

For nearly three months more, Germany would continue to bomb Britain, and the pilots of Fighter Command would still be at the forefront of the island's defense. Londoners would still rush for shelter at the nightly wail of the air-raid sirens, and daily dogfights would occur over the Channel. But Hitler and Churchill both knew that the island kingdom was safe from invasion and that the Battle of Britain had been decided.

Despite criticism, Dowding's tactics had varied little throughout the battle. The accusations against him became even stronger after the fight was won. The charge was similar to the one that his reputation had so narrowly survived at the time of Dunkirk: that he should have thrown a far greater proportion of his forces into the day-to-day struggle, enabling the RAF to meet the Luftwaffe on more even terms. His critics contended that the margin of victory was narrower than it should have been and that by his obduracy he had exposed his pilots to murderous odds and nearly lost the Battle of Britain.

Dowding insisted that, had he thrown all his forces into the fray at one time, the resulting congestion on southern airfields and the overloading of communications and ground control could have led to early defeat. Furthermore, as at Dunkirk, he could not be certain how long the battle might last and thus had to husband Fighter Command's strength for a lengthy contest. The big-wing formations suggested by Leigh-Mallory, he maintained, were neither flexible nor easily controlled once they were airborne.

The controversy was never really settled; it still raged years after the War's end. But as far as Dowding was concerned it was settled very quickly. On November 16 he received a telephone call from the Secretary of State for Air. "He told me that I was to relinquish my Command immediately." The normal courtesies—such as a confirmatory letter with some reference to what he had achieved—were denied him. He was told he might make himself useful by "investigating service waste." Within a few days Park was relegated to commanding a training group. Sholto Douglas replaced Dowding. Leigh-Mallory replaced Park. After-the-fact analysis, largely sparked by Leigh-Mallory and Bader, had convinced the Air Staff that the battle had been mismanaged, and Churchill, impressed by the way Leigh-Mallory had led the northern squadrons, authorized the changes.

"Dowding and Park won the Battle of Britain," wrote the New Zealand ace fighter pilot Al Deere in 1959, taking firm sides in the dispute, "but they lost the battle of words that followed." ～

Images of air war

During the summer of 1940, one of history's greatest battles raged in the skies above England's densely populated southern counties, yet relatively few people other than the combatants actually witnessed it. All that most earthbound Englishmen saw of aerial combat during the Battle of Britain were wispy networks of twisting contrails as pilots fought for their lives some 20,000 feet above the ground.

Nor did the public get much of a view of the epic conflict through photographs. The Battle of Britain—unlike most major engagements of World War II—was barely documented by the camera. While German bomber crews sometimes took their own photographs of the action, regulations forbade RAF pilots to take pictures. When encounters with the enemy were unlikely, however, the British government occasionally did send up photographers to obtain a few pictures—like the one shown here—for release to the press.

Some aircraft carried camera-guns that automatically rolled motion-picture film when the weapons were fired, producing frames that, although blurred and grainy, are highly prized as part of a frustratingly sparse pictorial record. Despite their scarcity and generally poor photographic quality, pictures of the battle evoke the heart-stopping drama that was surely the RAF's finest hour.

A formation of Spitfires peels off into a dive, a maneuver used when swooping down out of the clouds onto an unsuspecting enemy below.

Dornier 17s swarm across the sky on a bombing raid. In the inset, an RAF camera-gun photograph, tracers find their target, a Heinkel 111.

In a photograph that was crudely doctored to emphasize the German wing markings, a Dornier 17 trails

moke in its death plunge. In the inset at left, a camera-gun mounted in a Royal Air Force fighter captures the fiery end of a Junkers Stuka dive bomber.

Hit by a Heinkel bomber, a flaming Spitfire (right) flashes past its opponent as the desperate British pilot seeks room to bail out.

3
Striking back with bombs

In a July 1940 letter to Lord Beaverbrook, Minister of Aircraft Production, Winston Churchill said that without an army capable of confronting German military power on the Continent, there was only one way that Britain could defeat Hitler. "And that," he wrote, "is an absolutely devastating, exterminating attack by very heavy bombers from this country upon the Nazi homeland. We must be able to overwhelm him by this means, without which I do not see a way through."

This was, of course, the very job for which Sir Hugh Trenchard had so carefully shaped the Royal Air Force and so rigorously defended it against its detractors during the decades between the Wars. Strategic bombing was the specific purpose for which RAF Bomber Command had been created. And it was an assignment that most of the present leaders of the RAF, Trenchard men who believed strongly that a bombing offensive would be the key to victory, eagerly wished to pursue.

It was to be a difficult and lengthy undertaking. To begin with, in the summer of 1940 the RAF did not yet have the very heavy bombers that the Prime Minister envisioned striking at the Nazi homeland. And before Bomber Command could launch a full-scale strategic offensive, its crews and the aircraft it did possess would be diverted to other, more urgently pressing tasks, on which the nation's survival depended. Even then, time and impetus would be lost in debate and indecision about what kind of targets the bombers should strike. Finally, when the chance to carry the War to Germany at last materialized, Bomber Command would be found wanting in the most basic aspect of its performance: its ability to hit the target with its bombs.

Bomber Command would eventually rise from this dismal failure to stunning success, thanks in part to technological advances, in part to the bravery of its crews and in part to a leader named Arthur Harris who was willing to gamble on a monumental scale and who understood that showmanship can affect the fortunes of war. Under his command Britain's bomber force would prove the validity of Trenchard's vision and its own ability to prosecute a devastatingly effective offensive. But before that triumph was achieved, the continued existence of Bomber Command would be seriously questioned, and even Churchill would wonder whether it was capable of doing more than merely annoying the enemy—and then only at great cost in British lives and aircraft.

Crewmen in a Stirling bomber prepare to embark on a night mission over Germany. Up front in the cockpit, the pilot starts the engines while the bombardier—who acted as copilot during takeoff—adjusts the flaps. The navigator (left) studies the course at his map table and the flight engineer (foreground) checks out fuses and switches.

Shortly after Churchill wrote his letter to Lord Beaverbrook, the Luftwaffe made its bid for air supremacy over England, to prepare the way for the German invasion force that was being assembled in France. As Fighter Command struggled to defeat the Germans in the air, Bomber Command was obliged to postpone strategic operations in order to blast the ground forces poised just across the Channel and to make strikes inside Germany that would delay the invasion build-up. In one such raid, Flight Lieutenant Roderick Learoyd won a Victoria Cross—among the first of 19 such medals awarded to Bomber Command fliers in the War—when he succeeded in hitting an aqueduct on the Dortmund-Ems canal from the nearly suicidal level of only 150 feet. The canal was blocked for 10 days, throwing the Germans seriously behind schedule in the movement of boats and barges to the invasion ports.

But still a German amphibious attack seemed inevitable. On the 7th of September, Alert No. 1 was issued: "Invasion imminent, and probable within 12 hours." The fears were justified. It was not yet clear whether Fighter Command would beat back the Luftwaffe, and Channel ports in France were filled with more than

Dwarfed by a Stirling heavy bomber they manned and supported, 56 RAF personnel stand grouped by specialty. Behind the plane's eight-man air crew are the 48 members of the squadron's ground staff, including a WAAF parachute packer (third row, center) and, behind the trolley of bombs, the 11-man bomb-loading team.

1,000 barges waiting to ferry German troops to Britain's shores.

To counter this threat, all of Bomber Command was mustered to attack the invasion fleet. Night after night the bombers flew over the invasion assembly areas on the French coast west of Dunkirk. One pilot recalled feeling that "there was not enough night to do as many trips as we wanted—that was the sense of urgency we had." Another pilot, Flying Officer R. S. Gilmour, looked out his window and saw a spectacle unlike any he had seen before: "Calais docks were on fire. So was the waterfront of Boulogne, and glares extended for miles. The whole French coast seemed to be a barrier of flame broken only by intense white flashes of exploding bombs."

In two weeks of intensive bombing, some 12 per cent of the invasion fleet was disabled. "The very severe bombing," noted a report of the German Naval Staff on September 18, "makes it necessary to disperse the naval and transport vessels already concentrated and to stop further movement of shipping to the invasion ports."

As time passed, the threat waned. A cross-Channel invasion was an awesome challenge—especially after the destruction of so many invasion vessels. And as the threat of invasion receded, Britain's Air Staff at last had a chance to order Bomber Command onto the offensive.

But now a disagreement developed. There were so many ways in which strategic bombers might attack the Germans and such limited resources for the job that opinions differed sharply about what form the offensive should take. Most senior RAF officers were in favor of hitting specific industrial targets, primarily in the Ruhr. But for weeks the Luftwaffe had been raining bombs on London; Churchill's government was under heavy pressure to unleash a terror bombing campaign on German cities to avenge the punishment that Londoners were suffering. "On every side," Churchill declaimed before the House of Commons, "is the cry 'We can take it,' but with it there is also the cry 'Give it them back!'" In the end, a rough compromise was worked out: Bomber Command would strike at specific industrial targets, but these must be located in areas of concentrated population so that even if the crews were not on target they would "demonstrate to the enemy the power and severity of air bombardments," and thus lower German morale.

Not long after this decision, Air Chief Marshal Sir Charles Portal replaced Newall as Chief of the Air Staff. He was succeeded at Bomber Command by Air Marshal Sir Richard Peirse, who was to implement the new compromise with attacks on Berlin, Essen, Munich and Cologne. Crews were told to seek a primary industrial target, then, if they could not locate it, to dump their bombs on "self-evident military objectives."

Terrible winter weather over Germany made the offensive sporadic and, to the extent that targets were obscured by clouds, ineffectual. But Portal and Peirse believed that when the weather cleared, the air raids would bite sharply enough to demoralize the Germans. Bomber Command's chance came on the moonlit night of December 16, 1940. The target was a plant in Mannheim that made diesel engines for U-boats. A force of Wellingtons marked the target with incendiaries, and more than 100 crews bombed the target area, leaving the center of town in flames.

There was euphoria—followed almost immediately by embarrassment. Reconnaissance photographs disclosed that many bombs had fallen wide of the target, some across the nearby Rhine in Ludwigshafen. Peirse blamed the operational orders, which he thought had relied too heavily on the accuracy of the marker crews. Recriminations had hardly subsided when Spitfires of the Photographic Reconnaissance Unit delivered a second blow to the command's pride. Pictures taken of oil plants at Gelsenkirchen, the object of nearly 300 sorties in preceding months, showed only a handful of craters in the target area.

Hoping to counter the depressing evidence of the Mannheim and Gelsenkirchen pictures, Peirse insisted that all bombers be equipped with cameras and flash bombs. Properly synchronized, the combination could photograph targets at night, just as the bombs exploded, and show clearly once and for all whether the bombing was accurate. Unfortunately, there were not enough cameras to go around, and the questions about bombing accuracy remained unanswered.

On December 18, the balance of evidence tipped slightly in Bomber Command's favor; an intelligence report indicated that bombing had reduced German synthetic oil production by 15 per cent. Armed with this estimate, Portal succeeded in persuading the Chiefs of Staff to abandon temporarily the compromise reached less than three months earlier. On January 7, 1941, they recommended to the War Cabinet that "the primary aim of our bomber forces during the next six months should be the destruction of the German synthetic oil plants," most of which lay in sparsely populated areas.

Before the campaign could be properly launched, Bomber Command was diverted to help blunt another German knife held at England's throat. The Admiralty began clamoring for bomber raids on U-boat bases in France and on shipyards in Germany to counteract mounting British losses at sea. Through the early weeks of 1941, while its Blenheims were diverted to armed reconnaissance duty in the North Sea, Bomber Command concentrated increasingly on naval targets. Finally, on March 6, 1941, after Churchill declared that "the Battle of the Atlantic has begun," more than half of the bomber force was assigned to the crucial war at sea; the rest was directed to abandon oil targets and emphasize ports and shipyards.

The U-boat peril—which Churchill later said was "the only thing that ever really frightened me during the war"—had not become critical until the spring of 1940. In fact, RAF Coastal Command was thought to have done reasonably well against the submarines, considering its largely obsolescent equipment. At the outbreak of war, Coastal had at its disposal 265 aircraft. But most of them were slow Avro Ansons, known as Faithful Annies for their reliability, backed up by a few Lockheed Hudsons and Short Sunderland flying boats. The command's

Clearing a sea-lane, a Wellington bomber with a two-ton electromagnetic hoop triggers a German mine fitted with a magnetic fuse. To be effective, such "flying magnets" had to skim close to the waves, but planes that flew too low were sometimes damaged by the mines they detonated.

"scarecrow" patrols—so named because they were meant to frighten U-boats into diving and thus interrupt battery recharging—were flown by unarmed Tiger Moth biplane trainers. Antiquated Vildebeest torpedo bombers were slowly being replaced by speedier Beauforts.

To make matters worse, Coastal Command at the outset of the War possessed no bombs capable of sinking a U-boat. The 100-pound bomb carried by the Ansons—optimistically designated an A/S, or antisubmarine, weapon—could not cripple a submarine even with a direct hit. This fact was clearly demonstrated when an Anson mistakenly struck the British submarine *Snapper* with such a bomb. It hit at the base of the conning tower; the total damage was four broken light bulbs in the sub's control room. The Sunderland's 250-pound bomb was more effective, but only when it exploded within six feet of the hull.

In cooperation with the Royal Navy, Coastal Command nevertheless held U-boats and surface raiders in check through the early months of 1940. It also helped clear the inshore shipping routes of the magnetic mines the Germans had started laying in late 1939. The job was assigned to a special force of Wellingtons, each fitted underneath with a magnetic hoop that detonated whatever mines the planes flew over.

But after Germany invaded Norway and overran France and the Low Countries in the spring of 1940, the entire Atlantic seaboard from Norway to the Spanish border lay in German hands. British sea and air forces available to protect the Atlantic life line were stretched dangerously thin. And the Germans were now able to range freely from their

French Atlantic bases over all the sea approaches to Britain, using not only U-boats and E-boats (39-knot patrol craft that fired torpedoes) but the Focke-Wulf Condor bomber. With a 2,000-mile range, the Condor could attack shipping beyond the protection of Britain's shore-based aircraft. And it could reconnoiter convoys for U-boats.

Worse was to come. In November 1940, the German pocket battle-ship *Admiral Scheer* broke out of the North Sea into the Atlantic, fol-lowed in December by the heavy cruiser *Hipper* and in January by the battle cruisers *Scharnhorst* and *Gneisenau.* Taking advantage of bad weather, all four slipped by night through the gap between Norway and the Shetland Islands. In the next seven weeks the two battle cruisers sank 27 ships, while the *Hipper* sank seven out of 19 ships in a convoy homeward bound from West Africa. Between June 1940 and March 1941, some four million tons of shipping were lost, more than justifying Churchill's alarm. Worst of all, the brand-new *Bismarck,* one of the world's biggest and most powerful warships, had just completed her sea trials in the Baltic. Hitler expected that when this vessel joined the two battle cruisers in the Atlantic, Britain would be starved into submission in 60 days. The British had to neutralize those ships.

The first opportunity came when the *Scharnhorst,* accompanied by the *Gneisenau,* put into the French port of Brest for repairs. There the two battle cruisers were detected by reconnaissance planes on March 28, 1941. In the first week of April, a total of 200 aircraft from Bomber Command attacked the ships; they failed to score a single hit. However, one 250-pound bomb fell near the *Gneisenau* without exploding, and the Germans moved the battle cruiser out of dry dock and into the harbor so the bomb could be defused without endangering the ship.

The *Gneisenau* was spotted in this more vulnerable position by a Spitfire on reconnaissance. At dawn on April 6 a Beaufort of Coastal Command managed to survive the withering fire of 1,000 shore and naval guns just long enough to plant a torpedo in the *Gneisenau's* stern below the water line, smashing the starboard propeller shaft. The Beau-fort crashed into the harbor; its pilot, a 24-year-old Scot named Ken-neth Campbell, was posthumously awarded the Victoria Cross.

On succeeding nights, British bombers finally managed to hit the *Gneisenau* with four bombs that did extensive damage to a turret and the gunnery and damage-control centers, putting the ship out of action for nearly a year. Though the *Scharnhorst* was not hit, her overhaul was delayed for crucial weeks because of bomb damage to the docks.

Now it was the *Bismarck's* turn. On May 18 she put to sea, and a reconnaissance Spitfire sighted her sheltering in a fjord off Bergen, Norway. She managed to break through into the Atlantic on May 24 after a naval action in the Denmark Strait in which the British battle cruiser *Hood* was destroyed. As for the *Bismarck,* damage suffered in the battle forced her to head for port. She shook off her pursuers and seemed likely to escape, but she was relocated on course for Brest by a Coastal Command reconnaissance plane. A torpedo from a Swordfish

Halifax bombers attack the Scharnhorst and Gneisenau in December 1941 while the German battle cruisers sit in dry dock at Brest, France, for repairs. After the ships had sunk or captured 22 Allied vessels, the RAF's Bomber Command flew more than a thousand sorties to keep them in port.

flying off the aircraft carrier *Ark Royal* on May 26 crippled the *Bismarck's* steering gear. Efforts to repair her during the night were fruitless, and morning found her almost helpless as the British battleships *King George V* and *Rodney* bore in from the northwest. Shortly before 9 a.m. the two vessels opened fire on the *Bismarck,* and were soon joined by two more British warships. As the range closed to two miles, round after round battered the German battleship. About 90 minutes after the first shot was fired, the *Bismarck* sank.

Not three weeks later, intelligence reports indicated that the German pocket battleship *Lützow* had left Kiel Bay in the Baltic and was steaming toward the shelter of the Trondheim fjords. Shortly before midnight on June 12, a torpedo strike force of 14 Coastal Command Beauforts took off from Scotland in search of the ship. The formation became split up in low clouds and rain squalls, and Flight Sergeant R. H. Loveitt was alone when he spotted the moonlit *Lützow* through a break in the clouds. He raced across the stern of an attendant destroyer and launched his torpedo with deadly precision. The stricken *Lützow* limped back to Kiel and stayed in dry dock there for the next six months. In the two months or so since the attacks on the *Gneisenau,* four major German warships had been sunk or incapacitated.

In the second half of 1941 Bomber Command carried out a grueling campaign against enemy shipping. The targets were convoys carrying iron ore from Norwegian ports to Hamburg, oil from Spain to France and Germany, or stores from Hamburg for the occupation forces in Belgium and France.

The ships kept close inshore; as a result, the Blenheims found themselves bombing in the face of murderous fire, not only from the convoys but from flak ships, shore batteries and fighters. They suffered appalling losses. Flying directly into the muzzles of the guns, they would attack so low that their propeller tips would sometimes be bent from contact with the water. As a Blenheim hurtled over the wave crests, the pilot would shout "Now!" His observer would release the 250-pound bombs, and the pilot would wrench the plane up over the target ship's mast and streak for home, often weaving in and out between the vessels of the convoy, looking for a gap through which to escape the antiaircraft fire.

Many Blenheims crashed into the sea, and others did not clear their targets. One shaken pilot barely made it home after smashing through the rigging of a German ship; a mast ripped open his plane's transparent plastic nose, killing his observer. In one month alone, Bomber Command lost 23 of the 77 Blenheims assigned to antishipping strikes. On the average, a Blenheim squadron could fight for only two weeks before it lost so many planes and crews that it had to be withdrawn from frontline duty and rehabilitated.

Some of the pilots cracked under the strain: One veteran watched his wingman disappear in a storm of flak and then froze at the controls, circling the target aimlessly, unable to push his plane into a dive. He finally recovered his wits and flew home but never took part in another mission.

Still, by the end of 1941 Bomber Command Blenheims and Coastal Command Beauforts had sunk German cargo vessels totaling about 75,000 tons. In addition, the Germans had lost 137,000 tons of shipping to aerial mines—1,500-pound monsters that Bomber Command Hampdens parachuted into the enemy's shipping lanes. As Germany diverted more and more men and equipment to minesweeping and to shipbuilding and repair, the tide of battle gradually shifted in favor of Britain. Allied shipping losses reached a high point in April 1941—an appalling 644,000 tons—and then began to taper off. By July Allied losses were down to 121,000 tons.

Many factors contributed to Britain's success, the chief one being that since the beginning of the War a year and a half earlier, Coastal Command had more than doubled the number of its planes. Besides squadrons from Bomber Command, it got Lockheed Hudsons ferried from Newfoundland and new twin-engined Beaufighters—strong, fast aircraft with a range of 1,400 miles. In June of 1941 Coastal Command got its first B-24 Liberator, a four-engined American bomber with a 2,400-mile operational range, almost double that of any other Allied search aircraft. At the same time, Coastal Command bolstered its fighter cover for convoys by introducing CAM-ships *(pages 92-93),* merchantmen that carried a single catapult-launched Hurricane and provided a much-needed deterrent to the Germans' Focke-Wulf Condor.

Air cover was also improved in 1941 by stationing long-range planes at airfields in Iceland. British forces had saved Iceland from the Germans by landing at Reykjavik in May 1940, but it was not until the spring of 1941 that three Coastal Command squadrons were sent there to begin regular reconnaissance to the east of Iceland and northward along the Denmark Strait. The distinction of being the first aircraft in the War to capture a German submarine belonged to a Hudson of No. 269 Squadron flying out of Iceland. On August 27, 1941, the Hudson crew sighted the *U-570* breaking surface and straddled it with depth charges as it started a crash dive. When the plumes of spray subsided, the U-boat was seen again on the surface and several crew members were waving the captain's dress shirt in lieu of a white flag. Relays of reconnaissance planes kept the submarine under surveillance until a destroyer arrived and took it in tow.

More and better planes—together with improved air-to-surface radar for aircraft—forced the U-boats to retreat farther out into the Atlantic, where the Focke-Wulf Condors could not provide the reconnaissance support that had made the submarines so formidable closer to Europe. By September 1941, the German U-boat chief, Admiral Karl Dönitz, was complaining to Hitler of "the great difficulties caused by the very strong Anglo-American escorts and the extensive enemy air pa-

Caught on the surface by two Sunderland flying boats, a crippled German U-boat founders in the North Atlantic Ocean. Using a technique known as straddling, the Sunderlands had planted depth charges on both sides of the submarine in an effort to guarantee at least one fatal hit.

trols." The sea war was far from over, but Hitler's grand design for severing Britain's supply lines and bringing her to her knees in 1941 had been frustrated. The immediate crisis was past.

Bomber Command was now allowed to resume its strategic operations on the Continent, but not against oil targets. During the winter and spring of 1941, Hitler had stretched his supply lines by moving forces into the Balkans and Greece. Then, in June, the Germans launched a massive surprise invasion of the Soviet Union. These developments burdened the German transportation system to its limits and suggested to the British that strikes against transportation targets, with emphasis on railroads, might hamper or even cripple Hitler's war machine.

Since some of the most important rail targets were located in crowded industrial areas, the British could again select targets for their psychological as well as military merits, reviving the compromise that had been abandoned when oil plants became Bomber Command's primary objectives. "Our policy at present," said a report by the Chiefs of Staff in June 1941, "is to concentrate upon targets which affect both the German transportation system and civilian morale." These dual aims, added the report, promised that "the whole structure upon which the German forces are based, the economic system, the machinery for production and destruction, the morale of the nation will be destroyed."

Bomber Command now had at its disposal three new heavy bombers—the four-engined Short Stirlings and Handley Page Halifaxes, each with a bomb capacity of five tons, and the slightly smaller twin-engined Avro Manchesters.

At about the same time the new planes went into operation, the first real effort was made to measure the accuracy of bombing raids. Many aircraft were now fitted with cameras and flash bombs to take photographs at night of bombs striking—or missing—a target. David Bensusan-Butt, a member of the War Cabinet Secretariat, was given the task of evaluating some 600 such photographs, taken of railroads and other targets struck in June and July. On August 18, the Butt Report appeared, and its revelations were little short of scandalous. Only about a quarter of the crews claiming to have hit their targets had actually done so. Over the Ruhr, focal point of the new offensive against rail transport, only one bomb in 10 had fallen within five miles of its target.

The Butt Report seemed to threaten Bomber Command's very existence. Raids that missed the target were a waste of men and machines. Predictably, Bomber Command chief Sir Richard Peirse challenged the report: The sample was too small; the weather had been extremely bad; the photographs had been taken by inexperienced crews. For Churchill, however, the report only confirmed doubts that had been growing since the Mannheim and Gelsenkirchen photographs. "We all hope that the Air offensive against Germany will realize the expectations of the Air Staff," he wrote on October 7. But, he added, "I deprecate placing unbounded confidence in this means of attack." To Chief of the Air

One-way flights for seaborne birds

Perched above the deck of a merchant freighter, an RAF Hurricane such as the one below looked distinctly out of place, like a stray land bird stranded on a bit of flotsam. But for two years, beginning in 1941, these catapulted Sea Hurricanes, or Hurricats, proved to be an effective defense against the Luftwaffe's Focke-Wulf Condors, long-range, four-engined bombers that harried Britain's vital merchant shipping.

To protect convoys, 35 cargo vessels were fitted with 75-foot-long catapults and designated Catapult Aircraft Mer-

Propelled by 3-inch rockets, an RAF Sea Hurricane is

chant ships (CAM-ships). Because the aircraft could not land on its ship after a sortie, every launching from a CAM-ship was a one-way ride. Usually the Hurricat was so far from land that the pilot either bailed out over the ocean or stayed with the plane as he ditched it. If all went well, he then rode the waves in an inflatable dinghy until the convoy picked him up.

The CAM-ships were an immediate success. By the time they were replaced by new escort carriers, their Hurricats had bagged seven enemy aircraft and kept countless others at bay.

...atapulted from the bow of a CAM-ship.

Staff Portal he sent a message that Portal—a Trenchard man who believed strategic bombing was the key to victory—must have considered heresy: "It is very disputable whether bombing by itself will be a decisive factor in the present war. The most we can say is that it will be a heavy and I trust a seriously increasing nuisance."

Despite Peirse's denials, the Butt Report was correct. Bomber Command rarely found—and even less frequently hit—the target. The problem lay in navigation. Peirse's bombers were attempting long-range nighttime missions using navigational techniques better suited to short cross-country flights by daylight. Direction finding by radio signals broadcast from England could provide a fix for only the first 200 miles. After that, the navigator had to rely largely on dead reckoning. With a chart and a compass, he would plot a course based on the plane's speed and the estimated velocity of the wind. If the weather permitted, he might check his position by taking astronomical fixes with a sextant—a difficult feat from a moving aircraft. Otherwise his only way of checking his position was to search for landmarks, most of which were virtually invisible in all but the brightest moonlight. Under the circumstances, navigators were considered to have done well if they came within 20 miles of the target. Little could be done immediately about these navigational shortcomings, though Churchill backed Bomber Command's leaders in urging the development of scientific aids to improve accuracy.

Bomber Command faced more problems than that of navigation, for the Germans had been expanding and improving upon an ingenious night defense system that 43-year-old Colonel Josef Kammhuber began to set up in July 1940. In its initial form, the Kammhuber Line consisted of three small zones, each roughly 20 miles long by 12 miles wide, that stretched across a section of Holland from north to south. Each zone—the Germans called them boxes—was equipped with radar-controlled searchlights that locked automatically onto approaching enemy bombers. In addition, each zone had an Me 110 or a Ju 88 night fighter waiting to pounce—guided to its prey by ground-based radar. Behind the zones lay additional searchlights and flak.

The system's chief flaw was that the radar installation for each box could direct only one fighter at a time; nevertheless, it exacted a costly toll from the British bombers, which were usually widely separated by the time they reached the line on their way to the Ruhr. A bomber caught alone in one of the boxes and subjected to what the Germans called *Helle Nachtjagd* (illuminated night fighting) was almost surely lost. In late 1941, Kammhuber extended the shield to stretch in a crescent across all the Ruhr approaches, compelling the British bombers either to pass through one of the zones or make a wide detour.

What made the line particularly chilling to crews bound for the Ruhr was that they had to cross the obstacle twice, both going and returning. One of the more remarkable personal exploits of the air war occurred on a clear moonlit night in the summer of 1941 as a Wellington from No. 75 Squadron was flying over Holland's Zuider Zee, en route home after a

Bomber crews board their Stirlings at sunset for a night raid over the Continent in this painting by war artist Charles Cundall.

raid on Münster in the northern Ruhr. Detected by the Kammhuber system, the Wellington was attacked at 13,000 feet by an Me 110, and a hail of cannon shells and incendiary bullets set the starboard engine and wing on fire. The Canadian pilot, Squadron Leader R. P. Widdowson, told his crew to clip on their parachutes. Then he called his copilot, 22-year-old New Zealander James Ward, on the aircraft's intercom. "Jimmy—is there any way you can reach that fire?"

Gathering up an engine cover that was lying loose in the fuselage, Ward clambered out of the observation hatch into the slip stream. The Wellington had a lattice-like geodetic framework *(pages 44-45)* covered with a thin fabric skin; Ward kicked footholds in the side of the fuselage and climbed down to the wing. He clung like a leech to the wing surface, in which he made handholds, and crawled crablike toward the fire, clutching the wind-whipped engine cover under one arm. Once he was blown back against the fuselage and nearly lost his precarious hold, but he tried again and finally he succeeded in ramming the engine cover into the gaping hole in the wing and smothering the fire. Then he clawed his way back to the hatch, where the crew hauled him in. "It was just a matter of getting something to hang on to," Ward said later. "It was like being in a terrific gale." He, too, was awarded the Victoria Cross.

The Kammhuber Line and the growing effectiveness of German night fighters soon began to make Bomber Command's operations over Germany prohibitively costly. The loss rate—the percentage of planes that failed to return from each mission—increased from 1.6 per cent in 1940 to 4.8 per cent in November. A total of 107 bombers were lost in the first 18 nights of August. Then, on November 7, Bomber Command's blackest night so far, 37 aircraft out of a force of 400—9.3 per cent—were lost in raids on Berlin, Mannheim and the Ruhr.

Within a week of that disaster, Peirse was told to drastically reduce his command's activities and save his force for a renewal of the offensive in 1942. The Air Staff expected that by then new radar navigational aids would be available, more units would have been supplied with heavy bombers and the eagerly awaited Avro Lancaster would be flying. The new plane was an extensive modification of the Avro Manchester, which had proved disappointing because its two Rolls-Royce Vulture engines were unreliable and could not give the aircraft the speed, altitude or carrying capacity expected of it. The Lancaster, with four new Rolls-Royce Merlin engines, could fly higher and faster, with 14,000 pounds of bombs, 6,000 pounds more than the Manchester.

Early in 1942 Bomber Command resumed its duel with two old adversaries—with results almost as disappointing as its strategic bombing score. On the morning of February 12, two Spitfires came upon the *Scharnhorst* and *Gneisenau* with a screen of destroyers making their way at flank speed northeast through the Dover Strait. The ships had slipped out of Brest under cover of darkness and were making a dash for the Baltic port of Kiel.

Two flights of Swordfish and Beaufort torpedo bombers failed to penetrate the German convoy's dense antiaircraft and fighter screen, and all their torpedoes went wide. Bomber Command then mustered 242 aircraft, virtually its entire combat-ready strength, and launched a midafternoon strike. The mission was critically hampered by mist, rain and failing light; only 39 planes briefly came within sight of the targets, and none of them scored a hit. With visibility down to 1,000 yards, yet another torpedo attack failed. The German convoy slipped out of the Channel and into the covering night.

The press and members of the House of Commons denounced the RAF's performance as a fiasco. Bomber Command had not been able to hit targets 250 yards long in broad daylight on its own doorstep. Although later bombing attacks, after the ships reached Kiel, would permanently cripple the *Gneisenau* and immobilize the *Scharnhorst* for yet another year, that lay in the future. For the moment RAF critics interpreted the episode as a clear failure of air power.

At this low point in Bomber Command's fortunes, it got a new commander. Peirse was sent to command the RAF in India, and Air Marshal Arthur Harris took over the bombers in Britain. Harris was a man of strong convictions and iron will, whose blunt manner of speaking and talent for scathing invective had offended many in the chain of command. He owed his ascent less to influence than to sheer ability and tenacity of purpose. His tyrannical rule over his staff left little room for policy discussion or dissent. He was likely to reject curtly, though sometimes with a touch of humor, any opinions with which he disagreed. Once when deputy Air Vice Marshal Robert Saundby made some suggestions about alternative ways to locate a target, Harris scrawled across the memo the words, "Try ferrets."

Harris had one advantage over his predecessors: He had actually commanded bomber squadrons at various outposts of the Empire between the Wars. Air crews welcomed him as one of their own; newspapers nicknamed him "Bomber." He had the kind of resolution and drive that Bomber Command at this point badly needed. Just eight days before Harris took over, Churchill had authorized a resumption of the bombing offensive against Germany. Given a green light, Harris now had to prove what strategic bombing could do.

Harris was satisfied with the orders he received for the offensive. He would not be required, except in rare instances, to strike at small, specific targets that he knew from experience were all but impossible to hit under combat conditions. He was given the flexibility to attack heavily populated areas that also contained industry, an approach that Harris believed was the best way to destroy Germany's capacity to wage war. Bombs that missed the factories would still cause terrible destruction in the immediate vicinity. With adjacent buildings burning or in ruins, streets blocked by rubble, utilities disrupted, and workers and their families dead or injured, production in any factory would suffer, even if an air raid left it unscathed. Harris was free of scruples about bombing civilians who happened to be in the target area. No nation fighting for its

The steely gaze of Air Chief Marshal Sir Arthur Harris, the leader of Bomber Command, masks the genuine warmth that he felt for his men. Admitting that the missions he sent them on were like "never-ending games of Russian roulette," he said: "I am lost in admiration for them."

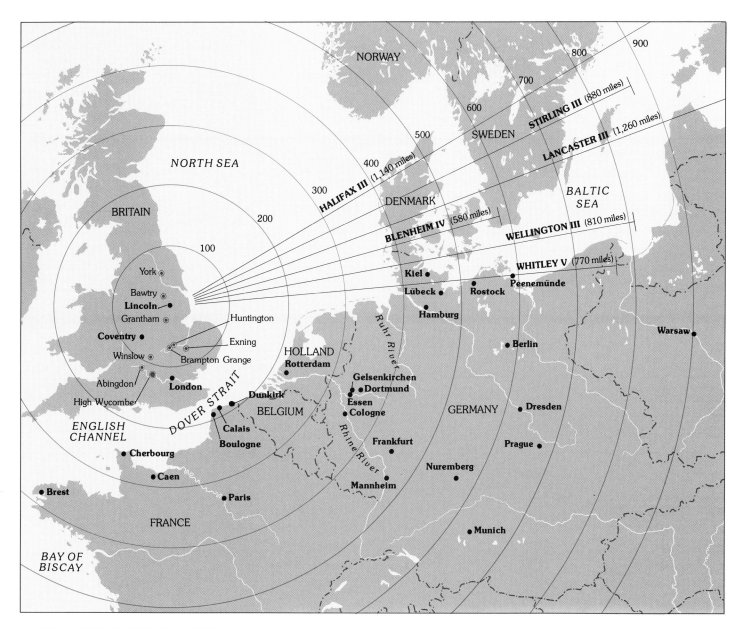

NORTH SEA

NORWAY

SWEDEN

STIRLING III (880 miles)

LANCASTER III (1,260 miles)

HALIFAX III (1,140 miles)

DENMARK

BALTIC SEA

BRITAIN

900

800

700

600

500

400

300

200

100

BLENHEIM IV (580 miles)

WELLINGTON III (810 miles)

WHITLEY V (770 miles)

York

Bawtry

Lincoln

Grantham

Huntington

Exning

Coventry

Winslow

Brampton Grange

Abingdon

London

High Wycombe

Dunkirk

HOLLAND
Rotterdam

Calais

BELGIUM

Boulogne

Cherbourg

Caen

Brest

Paris

FRANCE

BAY OF
BISCAY

ENGLISH
CHANNEL

DOVER STRAIT

Ruhr River

Rhine River

Kiel

Lübeck   **Rostock**   **Peenemünde**

Hamburg

Berlin

Warsaw

Gelsenkirchen
Dortmund

Essen
Cologne

Dresden

GERMANY

Prague

Frankfurt

Nuremberg

Mannheim

Munich

⊙ BOMBER COMMAND GROUP HEADQUARTERS
◉ BOMBER COMMAND HEADQUARTERS

*The combat radius shown here for each
of the major RAF bombers is the distance it
could reach with a maximum fuel load,
allowing a 20 per cent margin of safety to
make up for increased fuel consumption
in bad weather or in combat. When striking
targets closer to home, the aircraft would
carry less fuel and more bombs.*

life, he argued, could be squeamish about its methods. Besides, Harris
believed that bombing could obviate land confrontation and save the
lives of many thousands of Allied soldiers.

Despite his dislike for isolated targets, Harris scored his first big success by hitting just such an objective in occupied France. On the night of
March 3, at the urging of the War Cabinet, he sent 235 bombers over
the huge Renault motor and armaments works outside Paris. The raid,
favored by a full moon and perfect visibility, was a classic demonstration
of how precise bombing could be under ideal conditions. Virtually all
the planes reached the target; they dropped more than 460 tons of
bombs, destroying an estimated 40 per cent of the plant's machinery.
The morale of the bomber crews was so buoyed by the operation,
reported Air Vice Marshal R. D. Oxland, that "they are simply longing
for the time when they can have a repetition of this sort of work." But as

Harris well knew, the Renault raid, however important as a morale booster, was a subsidiary operation and peripheral to the main task of weakening Germany by bombing.

A team of researchers had been analyzing German night operations over England. The most successful attacks, they advised Harris, combined a generous use of incendiary bombs with a concentration of bombers over the target in the shortest possible time. To achieve this concentration, Harris was counting on a new navigation aid that in theory could guide a bomber to a target without visual fixes.

The system was called Gee, for the first letter in the word "grid." In essence, Gee transmitters laid out a radio grid across Europe, enabling navigators, through a cathode-ray tube in the aircraft and special Gee charts, to fix their position when they were at any point within 400 miles of the home transmitters. Accuracy at maximum range was within six miles. Until the whole bomber force was Gee-equipped, Harris decided to test the system by using bombers that already had it—about a third of the force—to identify and mark major targets.

The most tempting objective within Gee range was Essen, a dense industrial center in the Ruhr that was the home of the gigantic Krupp steel and armaments complex. If the bomber force directed its attack at the center of the city, it could scarely avoid crippling the Krupp works, which sprawled across the entire urban area. Gee-equipped planes would go in first and drop flares solely by instruments, deliberately avoiding visual fixes so as not to be misled by decoy landmarks. A second wave, consisting of incendiary bombers, would follow, and then the main force would come in, guided by the flames.

On the night of March 8, Harris launched the attack on Essen with 211 bombers, 82 of them fitted with Gee. The experiment was a failure. Many of the bombs fell on neighboring towns, and the Krupp works were scarcely touched. The first attack was followed by seven others of comparable size in the next two months, none of which did substantial damage. The hard lesson of these raids was that, while Gee could be relied on to find the general bombing area, it was not capable of pinpoint accuracy. Instead of putting their faith in so-called blind bombing, crews would still have to see the target.

Anxious to vindicate area bombing after the poor showing at Essen, Harris next turned his attention to the Baltic port of Lübeck. The town was not a major port—although it helped supply the German armies in Russia—and it had only a sprinkling of industry. But Harris was attracted to it because his bombers would have little trouble finding it; the port was distinctively situated on an island in the mouth of the Trave River. Moreover, the city's center, mainly medieval structures built of wood, was highly flammable and densely populated, and its defenses were light. He wanted his crews, he declared, "to be well 'blooded,' as they say in foxhunting, to have a taste of success for a change."

A force of 234 bombers, more than half of them loaded with incendiaries, struck Lübeck in three waves on the moonlit night of March 28.

Heavy "Stirling" bombers raid the Nazi Baltic port of Lübeck and leave the docks ablaze

BACK THEM UP!

A British poster designed to boost civilian morale shows Stirlings dodging flak and searchlights as they rain bombs on the German city of Lübeck. The March 1942 fire bombing of the Baltic port leveled half of the city; thereafter, in RAF slang, to "Lübeck" a target meant to pulverize it.

They were led by 10 Gee-equipped Wellingtons that could rely on their receivers to get them four fifths of the distance before they picked up the Trave River to lead them the rest of the way in. All the pilots were instructed to release their bombloads from the lowest possible altitude. The result was an inferno that obliterated the old town of Lübeck. Some 200 acres were leveled, 2,000 buildings destroyed and more than 15,000 people "de-housed," as the bombing analysts put it. Nazi Propaganda Minister Joseph Goebbels found the destruction "horrible," and he worried that such raids "might conceivably have a demoralizing effect on the population." In England, the raid was seen as a vindication of the bomber offensive and a personal triumph for Harris.

Harris repeated the performance a month later, throwing more than 100 bombers against the Baltic port of Rostock on four successive nights. Rostock, too, was an old, largely wooden city and hence a natural incendiary target. And the Heinkel aircraft plant was located in a suburb. High-explosive bombs and incendiaries wiped out 70 per cent of the old city, severely damaged the Heinkel factory, killed or badly wounded some 6,000 citizens, and caused civilians by the thousands to flee to nearby villages and towns. In the storm of acclaim that greeted Harris' latest triumph, few stopped to consider that both Lübeck and Rostock were special cases—meagerly defended targets that were easy to find and even easier to set aflame.

Attacks on other targets in western Germany proved less successful. Always sensitive to criticism, Harris now had to combat a growing feeling in the War Cabinet that in spite of Lübeck and Rostock, Bomber Command should perhaps be disbanded and divided between Coastal Command, the Army and the Navy. Harris decided there was only one possible reply to such a proposal: He needed a resounding victory over a major target, with a force big enough to raise the stature of Bomber Command in the eyes of the War Cabinet and to rekindle the enthusiasm of the public. He needed, in short, a bombing spectacular.

The largest Bomber Command raid on a single target so far had been the 235 planes sent against the Renault factory in March. The largest air raid in history had been a 500-plane attack on London by the Germans in 1940. What if Harris could double that figure and launch 1,000 aircraft into the heart of Germany? The number was irresistible, and Harris code-named his new project Operation *Millennium*.

To assemble 1,000 bombers for one mission was an astounding idea at that stage of the War—and at that point in Bomber Command's slow growth. When Harris mentioned Operation *Millennium* to Chief of the Air Staff Portal, he knew very well that he had only about 400 aircraft immediately available. He proposed committing not only the whole of this first-line strength but also whatever he could draw from his operational training units. The rest of the force would be made up of planes borrowed from Coastal Command. Portal was enthusiastic, and Churchill was so excited by the plan that he said he would defend it against any subsequent criticism even if the losses reached 10 per cent.

It fell to Harris' deputy, Air Vice Marshal Saundby, to put the force together. He pulled in all possible reserves, recruiting both instructors and pupils from the training units. Then just days before the raid was scheduled, Coastal Command abruptly withdrew from the plan. In the event, it mattered little. Bomber Command maintenance crews, working day and night to ready every available plane for the raid, pushed the number of serviceable bombers past the 1,000 mark. The selection of a target, meantime, had narrowed to Hamburg or Cologne. Both were easy to locate and not as heavily defended as Essen and other targets in the Ruhr. The final choice would be deferred until the last moment, so that the weather over the two cities could be taken into account.

Harris slightly preferred Hamburg as a target, but either city would give him an opportunity to test a favorite theory: An effective attack on a major industrial center required a concentration of bombers over the target dense enough—at least 600 planes an hour—to inundate the city's flak and fighter defenses. At the same time, he had a plan for breaching the dread Kammhuber Line. If the attackers all took the same route—instead of dispersing as they had in the past—and crossed the line in a tight mass, they would overwhelm the defensive boxes, each of which could engage only one bomber every 10 minutes. Harris called this steady, dense procession of aircraft a "bomber stream."

The attack was tentatively scheduled for the night of May 27; if weather delayed the raid it would be launched any succeeding night through the end of May, which was a period of plentiful moonlight. Harris insisted on maximum illumination over the target to ensure that all his crews, even the inexperienced young men from his training units, could find it.

Clouds covered the Continent on the night of May 27 and hung there for the next two days and nights. On the morning of Saturday, May 30, bomber crews at 53 airfields in Yorkshire, Lincolnshire, East Anglia and the Midlands were still standing by for orders. At 9:20 a.m. Harris walked from his office at Bomber Command headquarters along a narrow path lined by beech trees and down into the underground operations room. There he was told that although the weather over Germany was still unfavorable, the odds were 50-50 that the clouds in the Cologne area would disperse by midnight. The skies over most of the British airfields would be clear.

This, Harris realized, was his last chance of dispatching the force in the existing full moon—and possibly his last chance altogether. Should the target be covered by clouds, however, the whole operation might fail. If he ordered the raid to go ahead, Harris would be committing all of his forces, including his reserves, to a single throw of the dice, knowing full well that "our whole program of training and organization might conceivably be wrecked." Long afterward, he recalled the decision before him that morning as one of the toughest he faced during the War.

Seated at his desk in the operations room, he studied the weather charts while his staff clustered around. An aide, Group Captain Dudley Saward, remembered Harris' pulling a pack of cigarettes from his pocket, lighting one and pressing it into a stubby holder. Bending over a map, Harris moved his finger slowly across the Continent, bringing it to rest on Cologne. He looked up at Saundby. The raid was on.

The word went out to the squadrons at 12:05 p.m., and ground crews scrambled to load the bombs. As the tense afternoon wore away, the weather reports became more threatening, with visibility problems now predicted over some of the fields where the returning bombers would have to land. But Harris had made up his mind, and the briefing officers for the first time revealed the nature and scope of the raid to the air crews. The reaction of both hardened veterans and nervous beginners was much the same: They threw their caps in the air and cheered.

At dusk, the force—actually, 1,046 bombers—began taking off on a rigidly prescribed schedule, without knowing, as one chronicler later put it, "whether the disaster would fall upon Germany or upon Bomber Command." As the planes formed into a huge stream some 70 miles long that began winding across the North Sea, Harris got into his Bentley and drove over to Chequers, the Prime Minister's country house. Churchill had invited him to dine that evening with Henry H. "Hap" Arnold, commanding general of the United States Army Air Forces.

Over the North Sea, the bombers ran into thick clouds that coated their wings with ice, but the sky began to clear as they thundered over Holland. More than 100 of the older planes had to turn back because of icing or mechanical difficulties, and Me 110s and Ju 88s shot down a few over Holland, at the Kammhuber Line. But to ensure that German night fighters would be kept busy, Harris had arranged for 88 light bombers and fighters to make diversionary incursions over airfields in France, Belgium, Holland and Germany, and the bulk of the bomber stream arrived over the target intact, eight minutes ahead of schedule. At 12:47 a.m. the bombs began to fall on Cologne.

The plan called for Gee-equipped Wellingtons in the vanguard to drop incendiaries for the first 15 minutes. They were followed by the medium bombers, dropping high-explosive bombs as well as incendiaries. The final wave consisted of the heavy bombers—Lancasters and Halifaxes—which were supposed to pulverize what was left of the city with 1,000- and 4,000-pound bombs. They used a variety of aiming points to spread the devastation as widely as possible, and they bombed at heights chosen by the group commanders—but not lower than 8,000 feet, in order to avoid flak. All planes were to head for home 90 minutes after zero hour, whether or not they had dropped their bombs.

As Harris had anticipated, the fighters and antiaircraft gunners defending Cologne were overwhelmed and could offer only sporadic resistance. So devastating were the early incendiary attacks that from a great distance away crews toward the rear of the bomber stream began to see a glow that they thought was a great forest fire. Only as they drew near did they perceive that it was the burning city.

Many planes circling over the heart of the city were hard put to find an area that still seemed worth dumping their bombs on. Every section

appeared to be aflame—from the docks on the Rhine River to the jumble of old buildings around the twin towers of Cologne's 700-year-old cathedral. All told, 600 acres were devastated, 12,000 fires started, 250 factories and more than 18,000 other structures seriously damaged or destroyed. Some 45,000 people were left homeless. Considering the extent of the destruction, however, casualties were surprisingly light. According to a tally by the Cologne police, about 5,000 people were injured and fewer than 500 killed.

Losses to Bomber Command were far fewer than many had feared. Forty aircraft, 3.8 per cent of those that had begun the raid, did not return. This was a considerably lower loss rate than the 4.6 per cent averaged on moonlit raids over western Germany. Most of the planes downed over Cologne had been hit by flak; only two collided.

But 116 aircraft were seriously damaged, and some of them barely made it home. A Manchester flown by Flight Sergeant Tolley Taylor was hit by flak that set the starboard engine on fire. Taylor sent the plane into a steep dive in the desperate hope that the slip stream might blow out the flames. He pulled out at 9,000 feet and at first ordered the crew to bail out but as the fire flickered and died he changed his mind. Instead they jettisoned guns, ammunition, armor and a portable toilet and limped home on one engine. Less lucky was 20-year-old Flying Officer Leslie Manser, who had to make his bombing run at a mere 7,000 feet because of overheating engines. Hit by flak and with an engine in flames, the plane began losing altitude over Belgium on the way back to England. Manser remained at the controls to give his crew a chance to bail out but then had no time to escape himself. He crashed with his plane and was posthumously awarded the Victoria Cross.

The morning after the raid, four reconnaissance planes flew over Cologne but were unable to take pictures because of the dense smoke. As later reconnaissance flights revealed the extent of the damage, Churchill was elated. "This proof of the growing power of the British bomber force," he wrote Harris, "is also the herald of what Germany will receive, city by city, from now on." The Cologne raid was indeed a herald, though not of the immediate future. Two subsequent strikes against Essen and Bremen, employing nearly 1,000 bombers each, had only moderate success. And as the weeks passed, it became apparent that the blow struck at Cologne had been less devastating than many at Bomber Command had at first assumed: The city was paralyzed for a week, crippled for a fortnight, disrupted for a month and seriously inconvenienced for much longer—but it had not been completely destroyed. The total devastation Harris dreamed of could not be obtained with the means then at hand.

Nevertheless, *Millennium* had a great psychological effect on both the British and the Germans. With it, Harris began forging the weapon he would use so successfully in 1943 and 1944. "My own opinion," he wrote later, "is that we should never have had a real bomber offensive if it had not been for the 1,000-bomber attack on Cologne." ➳

Near the twin towers of Cologne's majestic 13th Century cathedral, miraculously spared from major damage during the War, the ghostly shell of a gutted building bears witness to the city's devastation under repeated aerial attacks that included the 1,000-bomber raid of May 1942.

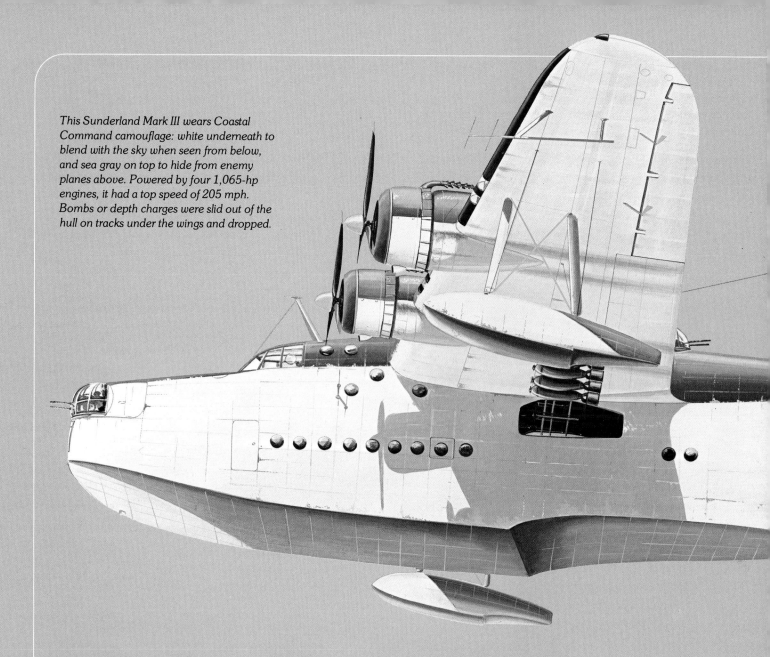

This Sunderland Mark III wears Coastal Command camouflage: white underneath to blend with the sky when seen from below, and sea gray on top to hide from enemy planes above. Powered by four 1,065-hp engines, it had a top speed of 205 mph. Bombs or depth charges were slid out of the hull on tracks under the wings and dropped.

A Sunderland copilot (right) uses a signal lamp to flash a message in Morse code to a vessel below while the pilot controls the aircraft. In the right foreground is a stack of signal-flare cartridges.

The flying porcupine

The RAF Coastal Command's Sunderland flying boat, built by the Short Company, was the nemesis of the German U-boat fleet in the North Atlantic. Armed with a ton of bombs and depth charges, it patrolled the sea for up to 13½ hours, escorting convoys hundreds of miles from British ports. When ships were torpedoed, its roomy fuselage and long range enabled it to save whole crews far out in the ocean.

When attacked, the plane was almost impregnable, as eight German Ju 88 pilots learned in June 1943 while trying to overpower a lone Sunderland limping across the Bay of Biscay on three of its four engines. In 20 passes, the Germans lost three planes to the Sunderland's seven guns, yet accomplished no more than to pepper the British craft with holes and kill one of its 13 crewmen. The five surviving Ju 88s, badly damaged, broke off the attack and fled in defeat. Warned of the Sunderland's firepower, German pilots honored the flying boat with the respectful nickname Stachelschwein—the Porcupine.

Hundreds of Sunderlands of four slightly different models flew in the War. Introduced in 1938, the plane was to continue in service for 21 years, longer than any other type of combat aircraft in RAF history up to that time.

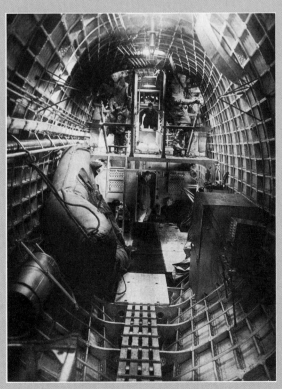

Inside the flying boat's cavernous hull, which could hold more than 80 persons, some crewmen relax while others (top) man the side guns. The rubber raft (left) was kept inflated, ready to pick up survivors from torpedoed Allied ships at a moment's notice.

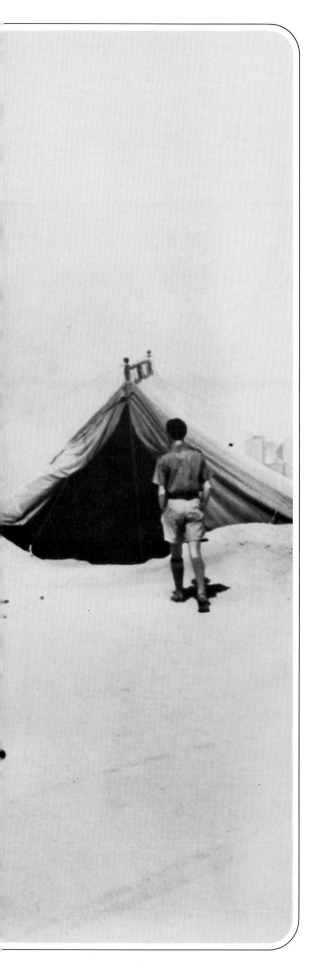

4
Defending the Empire's distant skies

Some 1,200 miles from Britain, Flying Officer W. J. "Timber" Woods and two other Royal Air Force pilots rose from the tiny Mediterranean island of Malta on the evening of June 11, 1940, to challenge an attacking flight of Italian Savoia-Marchetti 79 bombers. Flying outmoded Gloster Gladiator biplane fighters—the RAF's far superior Spitfires and Hurricanes were earmarked at the time for the defense of England—the three Britons engaged the first wave of five enemy bombers and drove them back out to sea. Then the Gladiators wheeled to face another five-plane Italian formation that was droning toward the key port city of Valletta.

Timber Woods, flying at about 11,000 feet, got in one good burst of machine-gun fire before the swift, trimotored SM.79s left him behind and proceeded with their mission. And then Woods heard the unmistakable chatter of machine guns coming from behind his plane. Banking sharply to his left, he saw that he was being pursued by a Macchi-Castoldi 200, Italy's foremost fighter plane. Woods threw his Gladiator into a tight circle, trying desperately to evade the enemy's guns. The maneuver worked even better than he had hoped: He found the Italian fighter in his sights and squeezed off a rapid burst of fire. The enemy went into a steep dive, trailing a plume of thick black smoke. "I could not follow him down," wrote Woods in his combat report that night, "but he appeared to go into the sea."

Woods's victory was the first of many to be won by British fliers based far from the main scene of conflict. Throughout the War, while RAF pilots first battled for the life of Britain in the skies over their beleaguered island nation and then pounded at the heartland of the German Reich, British fliers in other quarters of the globe fought just as desperately to maintain vital shipping routes, to strangle enemy supply lines and to defend their far-flung Empire from the onslaughts of its foes. First on the island stronghold of Malta and in North Africa and then in distant Asia, they would take to the air in whatever planes they could muster.

The Italian assault on Malta had been only the prelude to a much larger battle. Benito Mussolini had declared war on Britain and France only the day before, and the attack on Malta was his first belligerent act.

As pilots in desert uniform look on, a Hurricane prepares for takeoff at an RAF airfield in Egypt. Far from the European theater, North Africa was one of many key outposts manned by the RAF.

The island, located just 60 miles south of Sicily, was an inviting target. But Mussolini's real goal was North Africa, where he dreamed of establishing himself as a latter-day Caesar, building a new Roman Empire that would dominate the Mediterranean. Already, he had sent 215,000 men and 280 aircraft to the Italian colony of Libya. When the German conquest of France removed any threat to Libya from its western neighbor, French Tunisia, Italian troops began assembling near Libya's eastern border, only a few miles from British-protected Egypt.

The defense of Egypt, the Suez Canal and the Persian Gulf area—with its rich reserves of oil—and the maintenance of sea-lanes to British possessions in Asia, were vital to Britain's war effort. Much of the responsibility for this defense would fall to RAF units operating under the sprawling Middle East Command, which covered an area of 4.5 million square miles stretching from Egypt through Palestine, Jordan and Iraq to the east, north to Cyprus, Turkey, Greece and the Balkans, and south through the Sudan to Ethiopia, Somaliland and Kenya. But when the opening guns sounded in Mussolini's bid for control of North Africa, the RAF leader in Middle East Command, Air Chief Marshal Sir Arthur Longmore, had a mere 300 aircraft at his disposal, most of them outdated and about half of them concentrated in Egypt.

Malta, sitting strategically along Italy's main supply route to North Africa, was probably the worst-equipped of all RAF outposts in the Mediterranean region. Four Hurricane squadrons scheduled to defend the island had never been sent; the only serviceable fighters on hand—accidentally left behind by an aircraft carrier and hastily assembled for the defense of Malta—were the Gladiators flown by Timber Woods and his fellow pilots to confront the first Italian raiders. Later nicknamed Faith, Hope and Charity, the three Gladiators mounted such a vigorous defense that enemy pilots estimated Malta's fighter strength at 25 aircraft. Even so, the raids continued, and after two weeks of bombardment the propagandists of Radio Berlin declared that Germany's Italian allies had "completely destroyed" the British base at Malta. But when the Italians sought to obtain photographs of this triumph, their reconnaissance plane was shot down by the island's defenders.

At the end of June, four Hurricane fighters joined the three Gladiators on Malta. A dozen more Hurricanes arrived in August and were followed by a number of bombers. The planes would be sorely needed to support the British campaign in North Africa. On September 13, Italian troops swarmed into Egypt from Libya; three days later they reached the coastal city of Sidi Barrani, 60 miles inside Egypt, where they paused to await supplies. The British defenders, led by General Sir Archibald Wavell and supported by RAF units under Canadian Air Commodore Raymond Collishaw, Britain's second-ranking fighter ace of World War I, fell back to prepared positions at Mersa Matruh, 80 miles to the east.

It was a critical juncture in the battle for North Africa. The British feared that Hitler might come to Mussolini's aid and eagerly sought to defeat the Italian armies before German help could intervene. In preparation for Wavell's planned offensive, RAF long-range bombers from Malta and from the Suez Canal area struck at enemy ports, airfields and lines of communication, sometimes against stiff opposition. Alexander Clifford, a war correspondent who went along on an RAF night mission against enemy port facilities, wrote that "showers of tracers met us and barred the way" to the target. But the pilot found another angle from which to make his attack. As the plane made its third and last bombing pass over the target area, Clifford recorded, "the result was spectacular. A large barn-like building flashed into orange flame, and its roof soared gently upward, then fell back in fragments. Swirls of white smoke spiralled up, and as we swung away out to sea I saw two more explosions."

Wavell's Thirty Thousand, as they came to be called, set off to close the 80-mile gap between the two armies on the night of December 7, 1940, and within two months they had pushed more than 500 miles to Benghazi, Libya, and beyond, routing nine Italian divisions and capturing 130,000 prisoners.

Not once in Wavell's eight-week campaign were British troops seriously delayed by enemy air attack. In France the troops had often wondered what had happened to the RAF, and similar comments at first were heard in the desert. But such complaints were soon stilled. Once, as the men in a British ground unit watched an approaching squadron of Savoia-Marchetti 79 bombers and their escorting fighters, RAF fighters suddenly appeared in the sky. "In the space of a few minutes," one soldier recalled later, "four Savoias and four fighters were on the ground. Soldiers stood and cheered, throwing anything into the air they could lay their hands on." The RAF not only gave unstinted support but was seen to do so, which had rarely happened at Dunkirk.

Despite Wavell's successes, the battle for North Africa was far from over. On February 12, 1941, a German armored force under General Erwin Rommel arrived in Tripoli to reinforce the Italians and stabilize the Axis position in Libya. Rommel opened his offensive six weeks later, and by April 13 he had driven Wavell to the Egyptian frontier, clearing all of Libya except the British coastal stronghold of Tobruk.

Wavell's aim to eliminate the Italians before German troops reached North Africa—and his subsequent effort to hold out against Rommel—had been frustrated by Churchill's decision to divert British forces to a new crisis area, Greece. Mussolini had invaded Greece from Italian-occupied Albania on October 28, 1940. Britain was pledged to support the Greeks, and while Longmore was conscious of the danger of further dispersing his meager Middle East Command forces, at Churchill's insistence he at once dispatched a squadron of Blenheims, half of them converted from bombers to fighters, and he soon sent two more standard Blenheim bomber squadrons and a squadron of Gladiator fighters.

When RAF crews arrived in Greece, they were mobbed in the streets and carried on the shoulders of cheering citizens, who saw the British as the saviors of their country. The joy of the Greeks was premature, however. The Blenheim fighters kept Italian bombers from attacking

Smaller than London, the 95-square-mile island of Malta was a vital base for British air operations during World War II.

RAF Hurricanes take to the sky from Malta to intercept Italian bombers. In all, enemy planes dropped 16,000 tons of bombs on the island.

Lying between the Axis territories of Sicily and Libya, Malta occupied a strategic position in the Mediterranean. Though the island fortress was blockaded by air and sea for much of the War, its RAF squadrons mounted an aerial offensive of their own against enemy strongholds.

Athens, and the Gladiators, operating closer to the front lines, destroyed many of the enemy aircraft. But the British bombers, outnumbered and handicapped by airfields that were often waterlogged by winter rains, could do little more than harass the invading forces.

Then on April 6, the Germans crossed the Bulgarian frontier to assist their Italian allies, and the overpowered RAF suffered much the same fate that had overtaken it in France a year before. At times, entire flights were wiped out. For instance, on April 13—Easter Sunday—six Blenheim bombers of No. 211 Squadron sent to attack advancing German troops on the Florina-Monastir road, near the Greek-Yugoslav border, were shot down, and only two of the 18 crewmen survived.

Even the most skillful fighter pilots fared little better, but things soon improved when one of them, South African Squadron Leader Marmaduke T. St. John "Pat" Pattle arrived in Greece after distinguishing himself in the desert war, and took command of No. 33 Squadron. Equipped with swift and nimble Hurricanes and led by the resourceful Pattle, the squadron fought against great odds and averaged five enemy planes for every Hurricane shot down.

But this was not enough. With no replacements, the number of Hurricanes in Greece was reduced by April 22 to a mere 14, which were gathered together for a last desperate attempt to keep the skies clear during the final retreat in the face of overwhelming enemy forces. On that day, Pattle led his Hurricanes straight into a cluster of German fighters. With his first burst he destroyed a Messerschmitt 110; he selected a second 110, and this too fell in flames. Then he was chased by two Me 109s, which he avoided in a tight turn. His evasive action fortuitously brought him into position to fire at another 109, which exploded in mid-air. He swung around to help a comrade who was being chased by a 110. Pattle was about to open fire when two other 110s pounced on him and sent him crashing to his death.

By the beginning of May, the British forces had been evacuated from Greece by sea, some to North Africa and some to the Mediterranean island of Crete, where a dozen or so Hurricanes and Gladiators were all that stood between the RAF and the Luftwaffe—which had nearly 200 fighters and more than 400 bombers based within range of the island.

Pattle's No. 33 Squadron, now led by Squadron Leader Edward Howell, was among Crete's aerial defenders. A seasoned Spitfire pilot, Howell had never flown a Hurricane before, but he got his chance soon enough. Early on the morning of May 14, just days after he had arrived by flying boat from Egypt, Howell was sitting in a Hurricane cockpit at Crete's Maleme airstrip, familiarizing himself with the controls. Suddenly, he heard the engines of two nearby Hurricanes roar to life and then watched as the planes rolled down the runway in a swirl of dust.

Howell started his own engine, and as he did so he was pleased to see that the mechanic who was manning the portable starter battery dashed away from the plane as soon as the engine caught. "This is efficiency," he later recalled thinking. "The boys run about their business." Then he saw that the mechanic had a more pressing reason for his haste: The airborne Hurricanes were already twisting through a swarm of German Messerschmitts, one of which was plummeting in flames to the ground.

Howell revved his engine and roared down the field in a hail of bullets sprayed by the attacking Me 109s. Unscathed, he lifted from the runway and went immediately into an evasive turn, his wing tip nearly dragging on the ground. Alone in a strange plane, he groped for handles and switches to retract his landing gear, close his canopy, turn on his gunsight and activate the firing button—all while his too-large, borrowed flying helmet kept slipping over his eyes. In a few moments, having solved most of his problems, he turned to the battle raging around him.

Enemy fighters, guns blazing, were diving on him in groups of three and five, then soaring up and out of range of Howell's own guns. Howell saw two planes, one an Me 109 and one a Hurricane, spinning earthward. Then he spotted a pair of German fighters about a mile away, flying at about the same altitude that he was. He closed in on one of the unsuspecting enemy pilots from the rear. "I could have lifted my nose and touched his tail with my prop," Howell wrote later.

The Hurricane shuddered with the recoil of the guns as he poured a stream of bullets into the Me 109. Bits and pieces of the enemy aircraft broke away, and the plane plunged toward the sea with Howell close behind, still firing. He then pursued the other Messerschmitt, firing without effect until he ran out of ammunition and turned back to his base on Crete. There he learned that both of the other Hurricanes had been shot down, but not before accounting for at least four of the enemy.

The action of No. 33 Squadron that day was typical of the spirited sorties flown by Crete's doughty defenders. But the island's dwindling complement of aircraft was no match for the crushing numbers of warplanes the enemy could send aloft from bases in Greece and the nearby Dodecanese Islands. The RAF had only a few small and sparsely defended airfields on Crete, and its bases in North Africa were too distant to help in the island's defense. In any case, Middle East Command was too hard pressed on Malta and in Egypt to send fresh aircraft to Crete.

On May 19, the last seven operational fighter planes on Crete—four Hurricanes and three Gladiators—were flown to safety in Egypt. The day after that, German airborne troops landed on the island, which fell on May 31 after the evacuation by sea of nearly 15,000 British soldiers.

The twin disasters of Greece and Crete all but destroyed the good will of the ground forces that the RAF had built up in the desert war. The RAF had done its best against overwhelming odds but was roundly criticized by both the Army and the Navy for failing to provide adequate air cover for their operations. At least one critic, Royal Navy Captain Lord Louis Mountbatten, had ample personal reasons for carping about lack of air support: During the evacuation of Crete, his ship, the destroyer *Kelly,* had been sunk by a German bomber. Arthur Longmore, made the scapegoat for the affair, was relieved as head of the Middle East Command's air arm and replaced in Cairo by his former deputy, Air

Vice Marshal Arthur Tedder, who was promoted to air marshal.

Tedder was well aware of a "first-class hate" against the RAF for its alleged failures in Greece and Crete. But he stoutly maintained that wherever the RAF had been unable to operate effectively, the reason had been that the ground forces had lost the essential airfields. The enemy's air supremacy had made reinforcement in Crete impossible, said Tedder, and with no other bases within fighter range the RAF had been unable to prevent the airborne landings. Crete had finally proved that the prerequisite to all winning operations on land, sea or in the air was air superiority, and that such superiority could not be maintained without access to adequate air bases. So firm was Tedder's belief in this proposition that he declared: "This war is a war for air bases." This sweeping statement would soon be put to a crucial test where Britain's Mediterranean war had begun—on the island base of Malta.

In June 1941 Malta was reinforced by a squadron of Blenheims from Bomber Command's No. 2 Group, and Air Vice Marshal Hugh Pughe Lloyd was chosen to lead the RAF force on the island. His main task, he was told, was to sink enemy ships bearing much-needed supplies to Rommel in North Africa. Forty-three Hurricane fighters and 238 tanks had reached the British in Egypt by sea in mid-May, and Wavell was planning another offensive. Rommel, meanwhile, was being reinforced through Benghazi as well as Tripoli, and he still held the important Libyan airfields. Much depended on Lloyd and his Malta-based pilots, and he relished the prospect of attacking southbound Axis vessels. "The sinking of any of them," he wrote later, "might have meant the loss to the enemy in the desert of at least ten tanks, two or three batteries of artillery, one hundred motor vehicles and perhaps sufficient spares for one hundred or more aeroplanes, food for a month for one hundred thousand men and ammunition for one hundred guns for a battle."

Wavell's plan, code-named *Battleaxe,* was to push Rommel back from the Egyptian frontier to Tobruk; the British garrison under siege there was to break out and join the attack. For three days before the ground forces moved, on June 15, the RAF pummeled Rommel's lines of communication and forward airfields, and fighter cover was provided for the British advance. But the enemy still managed to put up stiff resistance, and the offensive quickly ground to a stalemate.

For the RAF, things soon took a turn for the better. An exhausted Wavell was succeeded as ground commander by General Sir Claude Auchinleck, whose appreciation of air power was such that he informed a group of his senior officers that the Army's main role in North Africa would be to secure air bases as far forward as possible. Then Tedder replaced his RAF field commander, the aggressive but impetuous Raymond Collishaw, with Air Vice Marshal Arthur Coningham, a New Zealander who proved to be a brilliant air-combat tactician.

In that summer of 1941 the Middle East Air Force was building up to a total of 51 squadrons. Curtiss Tomahawks and Kittyhawks from the

United States at last had replaced the aging Gladiators, but both were inferior to the German Me 109F, as were even the new Hurricane IIs that were replacing the Hurricane Is. With Auchinleck preparing to attack, Tedder could not promise complete air superiority, but he believed he could put enough planes in the air to deny it to the enemy. Auchinleck dared not delay; the longer he took to reequip and retrain, the stronger Rommel would become. From May to October, Lloyd's aircraft from Malta sank nearly 100,000 tons of Axis shipping, but German planes were also patrolling the Mediterranean, and the British were having more and more problems getting supplies to the vital island base.

Auchinleck began his offensive, code-named *Crusader,* on November 18, 1941, after the RAF had spent five weeks pounding at the enemy's positions. For a time, the Army moved forward unmolested by enemy aircraft, and one general, formerly a bitter critic of the RAF, said to Tedder: "I think your fellows are simply magnificent, and all my men are saying the same." But by early December both sides were swirling through thrusts and counterthrusts of inconclusive desert warfare. Then the Japanese suddenly struck at British possessions in the Far East (at the same time that they attacked America's Pearl Harbor), and men and

Raked by machine-gun fire from RAF fighters, enemy supply trucks swerve off a road in Libya during the autumn of 1941. The British kept up a relentless battering of German and Italian transport columns along this coastal road, which was a major Axis supply route through North Africa.

The shattered hulks of Axis supply ships lie beached in Tripoli harbor in this photograph seized from a German prisoner. Determined to destroy fuel and tanks bound for Rommel's forces, RAF bombers from Malta hounded enemy ships across the Mediterranean and into port.

planes previously intended for North Africa were diverted to Asia. The British offensive in the desert wound down and then temporarily came to a stop with both sides exhausted and short of supplies. But when an Axis convoy reached Tripoli in January 1942 Rommel counterattacked, regaining 300 miles of Libyan territory, including the important airfields and harbors that had been captured by the British.

The resupply of Rommel's forces had been possible largely because of the constant assault on Malta by German bombers based in nearby Sicily. Malta's effectiveness as a base for RAF antishipping missions had been sharply reduced by the bombing. As the desert war once again became a race for seaborne supplies and reinforcements, the Germans had gained a decided advantage. And they meant to keep it.

Through the early months of 1942, German bombers droned almost unopposed over Malta and the surrounding sea-lanes until the island was threatened with starvation. Even when part of a convoy got through, bombers destroyed the ships before they could be unloaded. The airfields were pocked by bomb craters, and in February Lloyd was forced to send his Wellingtons and Blenheims to Egypt for safety. By the last week of March he was down to six Spitfires and six Hurricanes. On

March 26, Lloyd signaled Tedder that the "Battle of last three days has shown that Battle of Britain is nothing compared with it, certainly as regards being outnumbered and in having no reserves whatsoever."

And there would be no letup. In April, Axis aircraft flew nearly 5,000 sorties against Malta, averaging an air raid every two and a half hours. Me 109s hovered like vultures, swooping to attack whenever they saw an RAF fighter about to land. A British pilot caught in such a vulnerable situation had to abort his landing and take to the air again—with little fuel and no ammunition—and try to outmaneuver the German planes.

Despite the odds, the British fought valiantly, shooting down nearly 200 enemy aircraft in April. And when Tedder visited Malta that month, he was struck by the spirit of the island's defenders. "To see the morale of the RAF personnel is one of the most stimulating experiences," he wrote. Praise also came from the German commander in Italy, Field Marshal Albert Kesselring, who wrote: "The British fighter units deserve admiring recognition for their bravery, their maneuverability in action, and especially for their perfectly executed tactics of diving from a great height through the close-flying formations of bombers."

The RAF also deserved recognition for ingenuity. Once, when all of the British fighters happened to be grounded at the same time for badly needed servicing, a large force of enemy bombers and fighter escorts

Beside a wry sign proclaiming the capture of a German dive bomber, RAF ground crewmen paint their newly acquired Stuka with RAF colors and markings. By test-flying captured planes, British pilots gained valuable insights into the combat strengths and weaknesses of enemy aircraft.

appeared over the island. Knowing that the Germans monitored RAF radio frequencies, Group Captain A. B. Woodhall got on the operations room radio and began issuing orders to a bogus British fighter squadron, while a fellow officer sitting nearby responded as if he were leading the phantom aircraft and was about to attack the enemy formation. According to Woodhall, in the confusion that followed two bewildered Messerschmitt pilots proceeded to shoot each other down.

Ruses and determination could not for long blunt the German assault, and with Malta all but neutralized as a base for air strikes on Axis shipping, Rommel's supply situation had never been better. On the night of May 26 he mounted a new offensive in North Africa. But if the RAF on Malta was virtually immobilized Britain's North African air arm still had strength and vigor. As Rommel's columns advanced across the desert they were repeatedly slowed by waves of British bombers and fighters. Many fighter pilots flew five sorties a day, and Wellington bombers made nightly attacks against German positions.

Never before had Rommel's forces been pounded so heavily from the air. The RAF could not halt the relentless enemy drive, however, and as the British ground troops withdrew, Coningham coolly moved his planes to prepared airfields that kept his forward bases at a steady 20 miles from the onrushing Germans. Whenever RAF ground crewmen at one of these forward bases could actually see, with the naked eye, British planes bombing the advancing enemy, they knew it was time to move back to the next site. The shifts had to be made rapidly, with whatever equipment was on hand. Tedder, while visiting one forward fighter field at the height of the battle, saw 100 men bodily lift a damaged Spitfire onto a flat-bed trailer. "There was no crane available," he noted, "but they were determined not to lose the Spitfire."

Finally, in early July, Britain's desert force checked Rommel and held him at El Alamein, just 150 miles from the Egyptian capital of Cairo. Kesselring, rightly believing Malta to be the key to the North African conflict, turned his attention once again to the island, calling in almost 600 planes in a final effort to obliterate the British base. But Malta's defending fighter force had been stiffened, and Axis pilots found themselves arrayed against a fleet of some 100 Spitfires. After two weeks—and the loss of nearly 50 aircraft—Kesselring called off the mass assault.

When the German bombing of the island abated, RAF Beaufort torpedo planes moved back to Malta and opened a remorseless daylight campaign against Rommel's supply ships, while Wellington bombers fitted with torpedoes covered the sea-lanes at night. Rommel had set August 26 as the date to begin his final thrust toward Cairo, but that day came and went with no German movement: Rommel's mechanized forces were held up for lack of fuel. Two tankers were on their way across the Mediterranean, but both were sunk, one by Beauforts, the other by Wellingtons. Rommel was desperate. Early in the morning of August 30 he appealed for fuel and was promised that another tanker, the San Andrea, would set out from Italy at once, under heavy escort.

He decided to launch the attack that night, knowing that he would need the 5,000 tons of fuel on the *San Andrea* to maintain his offensive.

Later the same morning, a British reconnaissance aircraft spotted a destroyer-escorted vessel steaming just offshore along the inside tip of the heel of Italy. Overhead was a heavy Axis air umbrella that included a Ju 88 dive bomber and seven Macchi fighters. It was clear that this was no ordinary convoy. A short time later, on battered Malta, RAF Squadron Leader R. P. M. "Pat" Gibbs studied the reconnaissance pilot's report. Seeing that the ship's seaward side was protected by the destroyer, he decided that the best angle of attack would be from the Italian mainland itself. At 11:45 a.m., Gibbs led a force of nine Beauforts and nine Beaufighters down the runway and into the air.

The British pilots took nearly two hours to reach the vicinity of their quarry. Flying some two miles over the mainland, they banked and roared back toward the sea. The Beaufighters led the battle formation, fending off the Macchis, clearing a path for the torpedo planes. Gibbs, flying in the lead Beaufort, streaked low toward his target until he could make out every detail of the vessel, including its name, *San Andrea*. Finally, as the tanker's hull loomed large before him, he dropped his torpedo from 500 yards and lifted over the ship, missing its mast by inches. He pulled up steeply, dived on the destroyer and raked it with

Victorious Allied planes fly over the remains of Italian fighters lying outside their bombed hangar near Tripoli. Scrap metal from enemy aircraft captured in North Africa was sometimes shipped to England, where it was used to make new planes for the RAF.

118

A Baltimore bomber leaves a wake in the desert sand as it takes off on a raid over Axis-held North African territory in September of 1942. Built in the United States to British specifications, this two-engined light bomber was ideally suited to desert combat.

machine-gun fire before climbing away. Then the *San Andrea* lurched in the water and exploded in a thundering ball of smoke and flame.

Deprived of his promised fuel supply, Rommel had to call off his offensive; on September 2 he ordered his mechanized columns to retire from the field. Two months later, a final blow to German hopes in the desert was struck when a tanker that had managed to get within sight of the North African coast was sunk by Beauforts based in Egypt.

For the first time since the Germans had entered the desert war the British—now commanded by General Bernard Montgomery, who had replaced Auchinleck in August—had the upper hand. On October 23, Montgomery launched a decisive attack on German positions at El Alamein, and by November 2 the enemy was in full retreat. Then on November 8, Montgomery was strengthened considerably by the landing of large Anglo-American forces in North Africa. The United States had joined the war against the Axis powers following the Japanese attack on Pearl Harbor, and units of the United States Army Air Forces had already begun flying alongside the RAF in the desert. To better coordinate these joint operations, Arthur Tedder—who had been promoted to air chief marshal in mid-1942—was named in February 1943 to command all Allied air efforts in the Mediterranean theater, and the combined British and American air arms were soon harrying Axis shipping and driving the Luftwaffe from the skies.

The German and Italian ground forces fought bravely against mounting odds, but they could not withstand the combined power of the British and American Armies. By mid-May, all of North Africa was in Allied hands. But victory in Africa did not enable the RAF to concentrate all its energies against the enemy in Europe. For in faraway Asia, British fliers were engaged in a desperate struggle against the Empire of Japan.

On December 6, 1941, while the RAF was defending Malta from enemy attack, disturbing news had reached Air Chief Marshal Sir Robert Brooke-Popham in Singapore, the British island bastion that nestled at the tip of the Malay Peninsula. Two huge Japanese convoys had been spotted off the coast of Thailand, just north of British Malaya. It was clear that Japan, which had for several years been waging wars of conquest on the Asian mainland, was about to strike at Thailand. And there could be little doubt that the next targets would be Malaya, with its riches of tin and rubber, and strategically important Singapore.

Brooke-Popham, commander in chief of British air and ground forces in the Far East, had a plan for just such an eventuality. A special RAF force known as Norgroup would seize two key airfields in southern Thailand, thus denying them to the Japanese. But until the Malay Peninsula itself came under attack Brooke-Popham could only strain at the leash; the British Chiefs of Staff had advised him in no uncertain terms that he should do nothing that might provoke the Japanese. A preemptive foray into Thailand would be a clear provocation.

As it happened, war came soon enough. At 1 a.m. on December 8, a

Japanese battle cruiser opened fire on the northern Malayan port city of Kota Bharu. At 4 a.m. Japanese bombers struck at Singapore. Then came word of the attack on Pearl Harbor. (Japan's strikes against the British and the Americans were almost simultaneous, but at Pearl Harbor, on the other side of the international date line, the date was December 7.) World War II had become truly global, and Brooke-Popham was responsible for defending a vast area that included Hong Kong, Burma, Ceylon and the Indian Ocean, as well as Singapore and Malaya.

On December 8, the RAF effort was directed against an attempted enemy landing at Kota Bharu, where a squadron of Hudsons sank a Japanese transport ship, damaged two others and killed some 3,000 troops in landing barges. The invaders withdrew, but they returned the next day with reinforcements and soon got ashore—but not before a brave Blenheim pilot, his bomber ablaze from enemy gunfire, dived into a landing barge, destroying the vessel and all its occupants.

By the time Brooke-Popham was advised on December 8 that he could send Norgroup into action in Thailand, the Japanese had already occupied the crucial Thai airfields, from which they launched attacks on RAF bases in Malaya and knocked out all but 50 of Norgroup's 110 aircraft. Nonetheless, on December 9 three depleted Blenheim squadrons raided the Japanese-held base at Singora, Thailand, and while three British bombers were downed, the RAF destroyed many enemy planes on the congested airfield. Returning to their base to refuel and rearm, the British prepared for another raid, but only one Blenheim managed to roar into the air before a flight of Japanese bombers appeared and put the rest out of action on the ground.

Piloting the lone airborne Blenheim was Flight Lieutenant A. S. K. Scarf of No. 62 Squadron, a two-year veteran of Malayan service who had recently married an Army nurse stationed at the RAF base hospital in Alor Star. Determined to exact vengeance for the Japanese assault on his squadron, he continued toward Singora, 30 miles inside enemy territory. With the help of navigator Freddie Calder, Scarf evaded Japanese fighters until he was over Singora, where he dropped his bombs, dived to treetop level and then streaked for home. Gunner Cyril Rich fired 1,700 rounds at pursuing Zeroes, but the fleeing Blenheim was riddled with enemy bullets, some of which smashed the left-handed Scarf's left arm and plowed into his back. Calder and Rich held their slumping pilot in his seat while he flew the stricken bomber southward and finally set it down roughly in a rice paddy just 100 yards from the hospital at Alor Star, where his wife, Sally, was on nursing duty.

Carried into the hospital, Scarf remained fully conscious and even joked with the doctors as they examined him. His wife's blood type was compatible with his, so she gave her badly wounded husband two pints of blood in the operating room. Later, as she left the room, Scarf squeezed her hand reassuringly and said: "Keep smiling, Sal." He died soon afterward and was posthumously awarded the Victoria Cross.

Such valor and sacrifice alone could not hold back the Japanese

A life line over the enemy's heads

One of the greatest challenges faced by the RAF in Asia involved not air combat but air cargo. In February 1943, several thousand troops led by 39-year-old Brigadier Orde Charles Wingate slipped across the Indian border into the jungles of Japanese-held Burma, where they intended to disrupt enemy communications and supply lines. The RAF was given the critical job of sustaining Wingate's Chindits—so called after the Burmese word for lion—with airdrops of food, ammunition and medical supplies.

The seven roving Chindit bands were accompanied by RAF air-liaison officers who guided the lumbering C-47 Dakota transport planes to secret drop zones deep inside enemy territory. It was hazardous duty for the ground teams and the air crews. The Dakotas, which often had to fly without fighter escorts, were no match for Japanese fighter planes. Many flights were made at night to escape detection by the enemy, and supplies were often dropped from as low as 70 feet to avoid disclosing the Chindits' position to the Japanese.

As the Chindits advanced farther and farther into Burma—blowing up bridges and cutting rail lines as they went—air support and the Chindit operation became increasingly difficult. In April, Wingate ordered his jungle fighters to begin withdrawing to India. By the time the last Chindits straggled out of enemy territory in June, the RAF had flown 178 sorties and dropped more than 300 tons of supplies—all without a single casualty.

BRIGADIER ORDE CHARLES WINGATE

Soldiers transfer packages from a truck to an RAF transport plane bound for Burma to supply Wingate's Chindits in 1943.

Parachuted supplies drift down during an RAF airdrop to the Chindits during the spring of 1943. Food was packed in cans, each containing 10 days' rations for one man. The planes also delivered explosives, guns, ammunition, medicine and mail.

Surrounded by supply parcels for the Chindits, RAF gunners aboard a Dakota transport keep a sharp eye out for Japanese fighters while flying over enemy territory. Some airdrops were made within a few miles of enemy bases.

Chindits stranded in the Burmese jungle use parachutes from supply drops to signal, "Plane Land Here Now." The field was too pitted for the pilot to comply, but three days later, after a smoother area had been marked, he landed to pick up 17 wounded men and brought them back to India.

After recovering for four days at an Army hospital in India, some of the Chindits rescued by air from Burma offer a jubilant toast with bottles of beer. The jungle rigors had so debilitated the 2,182 men who made it back that only about 600 of them were judged fit for combat again.

invaders. On the day after Scarf's death, one of Britain's newest battle-ships, the *Prince of Wales,* and the battle cruiser *Repulse* were attacked by enemy planes in the South China Sea; 11 RAF American-built Brewster Buffalo fighters that went to the aid of the ships arrived just in time to see the *Prince of Wales* vanish into the sea. The *Repulse* had already been sunk. On Christmas Day, Hong Kong fell; Borneo was taken a day later. Malaya's ground defenders, meanwhile, retreated south through the jungle toward Singapore, with the Japanese in close pursuit. After more enemy troops landed in Malaya on January 26, 1942, the RAF moved its Singapore-based bombers and reconnaissance planes to Sumatra, leaving behind only a few Hurricanes and Brewster Buffalos for Singapore's defense. But with three of Singapore's four airfields exposed to artillery fire from the mainland, the last fighters were withdrawn on February 10. Five days later, the island fell to the enemy.

Malaya and Singapore were not the only targets of the Japanese forces that were based in Thailand. They also moved toward Rangoon, capital of Burma and gateway of the supply route to China. Burma could offer the Japanese a firm base for an invasion of India and in any case was an essential part of the outer defensive perimeter needed to protect Japanese gains in Southeast Asia.

The British had thought a land invasion of Burma unlikely, and its defenses had been neglected. At the headquarters of the RAF group based in Rangoon, a defense plan called for a force of 280 aircraft. But the only warplanes immediately available at the outbreak of hostilities were 16 RAF Brewster Buffalos and 21 P-40 Tomahawks of the American Volunteer Group, the mercenary Flying Tigers hired by the Chinese government. When Japanese bombers first appeared over Rangoon on December 23, 1941, these planes rose to meet them, inflicting losses on the enemy of nearly 5 to 1. But the Japanese had 400 aircraft in Thailand, and the defenders could not stop the bombers from getting through. Two thousand people were reported killed in Rangoon on December 23; 5,000 more died on Christmas Day. But Japanese losses were sufficient to bring a pause to the bombing.

Air Vice Marshal D. F. Stevenson, the RAF commander in Burma, had a reputation for demanding a sacrificial dedication from his crews. Now, fortified by a Christmas gift of 30 Hurricanes and a squadron of Blenheims, he sent the Blenheims within a few hours of their arrival to bomb the main Japanese airfields at Bangkok. The Hurricanes, meanwhile, struck at enemy bases in Thailand. The British soon destroyed 58 enemy planes on the ground, but the Blenheims had suffered so much wear and tear during their long ferry flight from the Middle East that they had to be temporarily withdrawn for reconditioning.

In the last week of January 1942 the RAF and the Flying Tigers frustrated a determined Japanese attempt to attain air supremacy over Rangoon, blasting 50 planes from the sky and permitting the safe landing of British reinforcements. In thus postponing the inevitable fall of Rangoon with dwindling and totally inadequate forces, Stevenson's crews and the Flying Tigers enabled the British Army to withdraw from the city unharmed. Stevenson then formed air combat units at Magwe, 250 miles north of Rangoon, and at Akyab, on the Bay of Bengal, doing what little he could to protect the retreating British troops. By that time, the Japanese were already in Rangoon, and the RAF mounted its last successful strike from Magwe: Ten Hurricanes and nine Blenheims caught 50 enemy aircraft on the ground at Rangoon's Mingaladon airfield, destroying 16 before they could take off and 11 more in the air. Then 230 Japanese raiders attacked Magwe, and the few British aircraft that escaped were blitzed in turn at Akyab. These two raids nearly eliminated the RAF's combat force in Burma, but unarmed transports flew several thousand refugees to safety and dropped supplies to British Army units that were fleeing north toward India.

During the rest of 1942, Japanese and British forces consolidated their positions along the chain of jungle-covered mountains marking the Burma-India frontier. In mid-February, 1943, a special force of British troops known as Chindits crossed into enemy-held Burma, where they were supplied by air *(pages 121-124)*. The operation boosted British morale, but its effect on the enemy was little more than a nuisance; a major, concerted effort would be needed to dislodge the Japanese.

Such an effort became possible in November 1943 with the forming of South-East Asia Command, under Lord Louis Mountbatten, now an admiral. The British and American air forces in the region were fused into one operational whole, known as the Combined Air Forces, with 48 RAF squadrons and 17 squadrons of the United States Tenth Army Air Force. The integrated force operated from 275 airfields and acquired a growing number of first-line aircraft, including B-24 Liberator bombers, Vultee Vengeance dive bombers, Spitfires and Beaufighters. It was subdivided into a Tactical Air Force and a Strategic Air Force. Transport units were combined in a Troop Carrier Command.

Early in November 1943, the new Tactical Air Force spearheaded a move by British ground forces down the northwestern coast of Burma while the Strategic Air Force attacked Japanese supply lines. The British Army checked an enemy counterattack, but then aerial photographs revealed that the Japanese were preparing to launch a major offensive against the Imphal Plain, which lay across the vital Allied lines of communication between Burma and India and was the site of six airfields and numerous supply dumps, repair centers and hospitals. The British forces, roughly equal to the enemy in infantry strength but stronger in the air, were determined to hold the plain.

The Japanese opened their offensive on the night of March 8, 1944, and made such rapid progress into India that the Allies had to airlift an entire division to reinforce the key city of Imphal. The move, starting on March 19 and including troops, guns, jeeps and mules, was completed in 10 days without a single casualty.

The airlift had barely been completed when the advancing Japanese cut Imphal's only land supply route, the road between that city and

Obscured by smoke, the locomotive of a Japanese supply train explodes during a low-level attack by RAF Beaufighters in Burma. A relatively slow propeller speed, close-fitting engine housings and specially designed exhaust pipes made the Beaufighter so quiet that many Japanese called the plane the "Whispering Death."

Kohima some 65 miles to the north. By April 6 Kohima was surrounded and soon became the scene of some of the fiercest fighting of the campaign. The defenders, adequately stocked with food, were provided with water, ammunition and medical supplies by airdrops made each morning by RAF C-47 transports (known to the British as the Dakota, the C-47 was the military version of the ubiquitous Douglas DC-3 airliner). The planes lumbered up a valley from a railhead at Dimapur, 46 miles to the northwest, and disgorged their loads from 200 or 300 feet in a blizzard of small-arms fire. Meanwhile long-range American fighter-bombers—Lockheed P-38 Lightnings and North American P-51 Mustangs—attacked Japanese forward airfields, and Spitfires and

Hurricanes escorted the transports and sought hidden enemy columns.

At Imphal, as at Kohima, the defenders would have been doomed but for support from the air. Both cities held out until the Japanese, lacking supplies and suffering heavy casualties, withdrew. The British were determined to turn the enemy's withdrawal into a rout, and the RAF stepped up its long-range disruption of Japanese supply lines and close support of British ground forces while continuing to airlift supplies to isolated positions. (Occasionally, friendly troops were killed when struck by airdropped supplies, mishaps that British soldiers wryly termed "death from flying fruit.") Now the Allies completely dominated the air and continually harassed the retreating Japanese. By mid-July, 1944, India was secure, and in October the British Army in northwestern Burma, supported by an Allied air arm that grew stronger every day, resumed its long-stalled offensive south toward Rangoon.

While the Allies had been marshaling their forces in Southeast Asia to save India and press the invasion of Japanese-held Burma, their forces in the Mediterranean were moving against the Axis on Sicily and in Italy, hoping to gain a foothold for the liberation of all of Europe. And just as air power proved to be the critical cutting edge in the East, the initial Allied thrusts in Europe were spearheaded by bombers and fighters.

On May 15, 1943, the Anglo-American air forces under the recently knighted Air Chief Marshal Sir Arthur Tedder attacked the heavily fortified enemy air base on Pantelleria, a tiny island—about half the size of Malta—perched in the Mediterranean on the invasion route between Tunis and Sicily. After 27 days of continuous air and sea bombardment that destroyed 40 Axis bombers and 196 fighters, the island surrendered. The Allies had lost just 16 bombers and 57 fighters.

After the capture of Pantelleria, American and British planes began a series of preinvasion strikes against Sicilian airfields, finally compelling the Axis air forces to withdraw their warplanes to mainland Italy. As the Allied troops began going ashore on Sicily on July 10, fighters from Malta, North Africa and the former enemy air base at Pantelleria patrolled the landing areas, and fighter-bombers disrupted enemy attempts to counterattack. The Allies lost nearly 400 planes in Sicily, but they destroyed or captured 1,850 enemy planes. Now the Allies had uncontested air superiority in the central Mediterranean.

With the conquest of Sicily, which was completed in mid-August, Allied air forces prepared the way for the invasion of the Italian mainland, pounding airfields, bridges, highways and rail lines. Then on September 3, 1943, four years to the day after Britain had gone to war against Germany, Allied troops set foot once more on continental Europe. On the same day, the Italian government surrendered.

Twenty months of hard fighting lay ahead before German forces in Italy would be beaten into submission. But while the Germans were defending Europe's southern flank in Italy, RAF Bomber Command was relentlessly carrying the War to Germany itself. ➤➤

A formation of RAF Baltimore bombers swoops down to attack a German division that is hurrying through the mountains of western Italy on September 10, 1943. The Germans were trying to reach the coast to repulse the Allied landing at Salerno.

On a visit to a fighter wing in Italy, Sir Charles Portal (third from left), Chief of the Air Staff, discusses strategy with his top officers, Air Chief Marshal Sir Arthur Tedder (left), Air Vice Marshal Harry Broadhurst and Air Marshal Sir Arthur Coningham (right).

Power for the offense

Most of the aircraft that served the RAF during the latter half of the War were expressly designed or modified to take the offensive against the Axis and incorporated improvements based on lessons of the conflict's early years.

Heavy four-engined Lancaster and Halifax bombers could reach hundreds of miles farther into Germany and were much more formidably armed than their vulnerable two-engined predecessors, such as the Blenheim and Whitley. Speedy de Havilland Mosquitoes fitted out as pathfinders located and marked targets for the heavies, as the new long-range bombers were called. The awesome weaponry of Typhoons made them ideal ground-attack planes to assist the advance of Allied armies, while Beaufighters struck at enemy shipping.

Of the planes shown here, only the Meteor, the Allies' first jet, played a chiefly defensive role, protecting England from V-1 buzz bombs. Aircraft on facing pages are in scale; the dates are the years these models became operational.

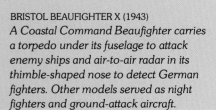

BRISTOL BEAUFIGHTER X (1943)
A Coastal Command Beaufighter carries a torpedo under its fuselage to attack enemy ships and air-to-air radar in its thimble-shaped nose to detect German fighters. Other models served as night fighters and ground-attack aircraft.

AVRO LANCASTER III (1942)
Lancasters like this one dropped 608,612 tons of bombs during World War II and accounted for more than 60 per cent of Bomber Command's total tonnage. The streaks on the plane's wings are residue from the engine exhaust stacks.

JA894

T4800

DE HAVILLAND MOSQUITO IV (1941)
*Constructed almost entirely of wood, the
sleek 380-mph Mosquito was unarmed
when serving as a pathfinder but was able
to outrun most of its attackers.*

HANDLEY PAGE HALIFAX III (1944)
*The second RAF four-engined bomber to
enter the War, the Halifax, shown here
in night camouflage, doubled at times as a
Coastal Command reconnaissance plane.*

GLOSTER METEOR III (1944)
This jet-propelled fighter could attain a speed of 490 mph at an altitude of 30,000 feet. The first Meteors went into service in July 1944, and some 200 were produced before the end of the War.

HAWKER TYPHOON IB (1942)
The 400-mph, heavily armed Typhoon devastated ground targets with its bombs, rockets and 20-mm. cannon. This one sports the invasion stripes it wore for quick identification during the Normandy landing.

5

A winged thrust at the heart of the Reich

Your primary object," read a directive to RAF Bomber Command in January 1943, "will be the progressive destruction and dislocation of the German military, industrial and economic system, and the undermining of the morale of the German people to a point where their capacity for armed resistance is fatally weakened."

It was a tall order but it brought a measure of satisfaction to Bomber Command's chief, Air Marshal Sir Arthur Harris. Less than a year earlier, influential members of Britain's War Cabinet, exasperated with RAF Bomber Command's apparent inability to drop bombs anywhere near a target, had given up on the idea of a strategic bombing offensive and sought to disband Harris' organization. But by rallying his supporters with the 1,000-bomber raid that flattened much of Cologne he had saved his planes and crews from an unsavory fate—assignment to the Army and Navy. Now Bomber Command, its image enhanced by the Cologne raid, had once again been given a vital role in the War.

The directive that crystallized Harris' mission was only one result of the Casablanca Conference, named for the sunny Moroccan city where it was held in January 1943. During 10 days of meetings, Prime Minister Churchill, President Roosevelt and the British and American military chiefs of staff delineated the pattern of operations for the rest of the War. This master plan called for the defeat of Germany, not Japan, to be the prime objective. And it was on a land campaign supported by strategic bombing, rather than on a bombing offensive alone, that the Allies based their plans for ultimate victory in Europe.

Bomber Command faced substantial obstacles in carrying out its assignment. The second half of 1942 had failed to fulfill the promise of the 1,000-bomber raid on Cologne. The effectiveness of Gee, the new navigational aid based on a grid of radio signals, was reduced in the course of the summer; the Germans had discovered the frequency the system operated on and jammed it. German night-fighter strength more than doubled, becoming the major threat to RAF bombers. German flak units, too, seemed to multiply like virulent bacteria. German fighters and flak claimed 1,404 bombers during 1942. Fortunately, British air-

Bomber Command crewmen of No. 101 Squadron await the start of a raid on Berlin in January 1944. By the end of the War, the RAF was attacking the German capital almost nightly.

craft producers were able to keep slightly ahead of the losses. Even so, combat-ready bombers remained too few and the bombing too inaccurate to inflict significant damage on Germany.

Never during the entire War would Bomber Command approach the first-line strength of 4,000 heavy and medium bombers it had hoped for, but this goal became unnecessary as bombing accuracy began to improve steadily. One reason for the improvement was the Pathfinder Force, formed in August under Air Commodore Donald C. T. Bennett. Initially, it consisted of the five squadrons in Bomber Command that had been most successful in finding targets. On future raids, they were to precede the main force at low level, illuminate the target area with flares, then mark an aiming point with incendiary bombs.

At the outset, the Pathfinders were only a qualified success. The fires they set to mark the target often spread, blurring the aiming point, and the Germans sometimes lit decoy fires to lead the raiders astray. The British retaliated with special target-indicator bombs that burst with an unmistakable—and inimitable—colored firework effect.

By the end of the year, the Pathfinders had compiled an impressive record. They accurately marked the target on 75 per cent of the raids they led when the sky was clear or partly overcast. However, when clouds obscured the ground, they had little more success in finding the target than the greenest crew. But help was on the way, in the form of two electronic marvels that were introduced before the

This wartime publicity photograph illustrates the RAF's awesome bomb arsenal. To ensure that no one underestimated the power of the weapons, a British Air Ministry employee scribbled the bombs' weights directly on the negative.

An RAF ground crew prepares to load the bomb bay of an Avro Lancaster with 1,000-pound bombs. Famed for its adaptability, the Lancaster bomber could be modified to accommodate the enormous Tallboy and Grand Slam bombs (opposite).

end of 1942: Oboe, a system that guided bombers by means of ground-based radar, and H2S, an airborne radar set that could locate a target through cloud cover *(pages 140-141)*.

As the Pathfinder Force sharpened its performance with the use of such devices, the rest of Bomber Command was being forged into a potent offensive weapon. Halifaxes and the new Lancasters, rapidly replacing most of the old medium bombers, were each capable of carrying more than six tons of explosives. Bombsights were improved and more powerful bombs were developed; by April 1943 bombs of up to 8,000 pounds were in common use. All these improvements infused a new confidence in Harris' bomber crews.

Thus, after three and one half years of war, Bomber Command was ready by early 1943 to shrug off past humiliations and to mount an air offensive against Germany with good prospects of success. Nor did RAF Bomber Command face this monumental task on its own. The United States Eighth Air Force was now in the arena, flying from bases in Great Britain. Though American bombers had not yet penetrated deep into Germany, they were preparing to do so, and the Luftwaffe faced the grim prospect of a round-the-clock offensive, with the Americans pounding away by day and the British by night.

To keep pressure on the Luftwaffe and to carry out the Casablanca directive, Harris was determined to hit Germany's large industrial cities, where bombs, even if they missed factories, could create chaos that would surely hamper war production. He resisted proposals to attack pinpoint targets, such as submarine pens, which required a bombing precision that was as yet unattainable at night, even with the help of Pathfinders. And bombing in daylight, though the Americans were determined to make it succeed, was still considered too costly by the RAF. In Harris' view, the strategy with the most promise was area bombing under cover of darkness.

The place to begin his campaign, he felt, was the heavily industrialized Ruhr Valley. The cities there were close enough to England, within Gee and Oboe range, so accurate bombing would be possible. But before Harris could act, the War Cabinet insisted that he adopt their priorities and first attack the German U-boat bases on the French coast.

The submarines were a genuine menace. But Harris felt that aiming bombs known to be inadequate for the job at submarine pens believed to be indestructible was a gross misdirection of his force, and such it proved to be. Of thousands of tons of explosives dropped on the U-boat bases between January 14 and April 6, 1943, not a single bomb penetrated the pens, which had roofs of reinforced concrete as much as 12 feet thick. Nonetheless, the raids were not a total waste. Maintenance and communications facilities near the pens were devastated.

When the antisubmarine mission was concluded, Harris once again set out to wreck the industrial base of Hitler's war effort. He opened the campaign by tackling the toughest of all Ruhr targets, Essen, home of the Krupp industrial empire. Not only was the city fiercely defended, it

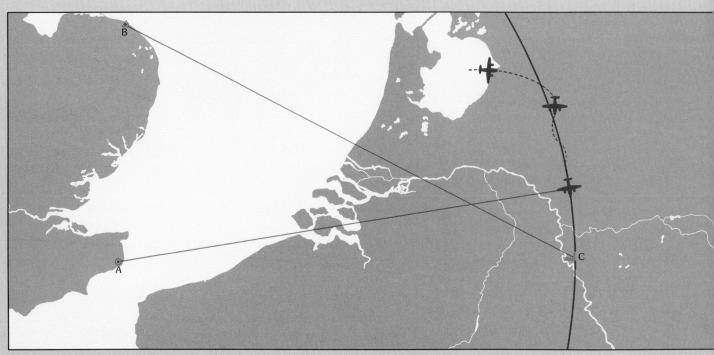

A bomber guided by Oboe flies along a circle centered on point A. The radar station there signals the pilot when he is on course. A second radar station at B also tracks the plane. When the craft reaches a prearranged distance from B, the station there tells the pilot that he is over the target factory, C, and should drop his bombs.

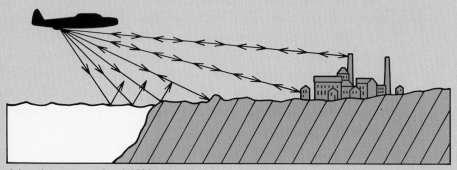

A bomber equipped with H2S transmits radar pulses earthward. Flat surfaces such as water send back few echoes, hilly surfaces somewhat more. City buildings reflect strong echoes, producing intensely bright areas on the radar screen. In the example at right, sea and lowlands show as dark areas, the city of Trondheim as a bright patch.

Bomber Command's deadly radar duo

Radar became a deadly offensive weapon in 1943, when the RAF perfected two highly secret navigation systems to improve the accuracy of British night bombers. The first, code-named Oboe *(left)*, used two radar stations on the ground to guide a bomber to its target. In one of Oboe's first combat tests, a raid some 200 miles from England, the bomber demolished the targeted building with a direct hit.

Despite its uncanny accuracy, Oboe's range was only 300 miles, and a pair of radar stations could direct only one plane at a time. Thus the system was used mainly in dropping target-location flares for large bomber forces to aim at.

The other radar device, known as H2S *(below)*, distinguished darkened or cloud-hidden cities from open countryside. Since H2S sets were mounted inside the bombers themselves, the system did not suffer the range limitations of ground-based radar. And any number of bombers could use the sets simultaneously, with devastating effect.

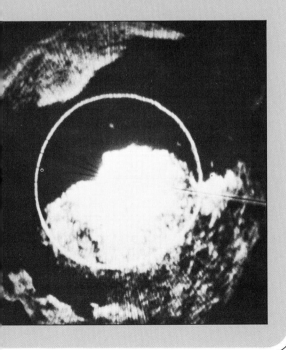

was also almost constantly hidden beneath a haze of factory smoke. On the night of March 5, Harris dispatched a fleet of 442 bombers, led by Pathfinders equipped with Oboe, toward Essen. By Bomber Command standards of 1943, the raid was a success. Almost one third of the planes dropped their bombs within three miles of the aiming point. More than 160 acres of Essen lay in ruins, and the Krupp factories suffered severe though not crippling damage. All but 14 of Harris' bombers returned safely from the mission.

Strategic attacks on Germany's cities continued, fair weather and foul. During the initial months of the campaign, the raiders continued to concentrate on the Ruhr, with only occasional forays outside that area so that the Germans would not feel free to pull in air defenses from elsewhere to reinforce the Ruhr. Later, cities in other parts of the country became the prime targets. The raids varied from spectacular successes to abysmal failures.

One of the successes was achieved on the night of July 24, 1943, when 791 bombers set course for Hamburg. On this raid, for the first time in the War, the bombers carried bundles of metal-foil strips code-named Window. Released on approach to the target, the bundles broke open in the aircraft's slip stream, creating a cloud of foil strips. The strips would fog German radar screens, concealing the bombers from radar-guided fighters and flak.

As Harris' bombers approached Hamburg from the northwest, they started littering the air with the foil strips. German defenses were thoroughly bewildered. One controller was overheard on the radio to exclaim in frustration, "I cannot follow any of the hostiles!" Mostly because of Window, Bomber Command lost only 12 aircraft while crippling Hamburg's municipal services and civil-defense organization.

Worse was in store for the city. Three nights later, 739 bombers carrying incendiaries ignited a fire storm that raged through Hamburg and incinerated everything in its path. Two more night attacks plus two American raids in daylight brought the city to its knees. By August 3 some 41,800 people had died in Hamburg, more than 37,000 others were injured, and two thirds of the city's million and a half inhabitants had fled. Albert Speer, Hitler's capable Minister of Armaments, told the Führer that a series of such attacks extended to six more major cities "would bring Germany's armaments production to a total halt."

Discomfiture, however, was not all on one side. German defenders quickly changed tactics to counter Window. Fighters, instead of being directed against a single bomber, were guided toward the bomber stream and allowed to find their own targets. British losses increased strike by strike. The Germans downed 17 bombers in the second raid, then 30 in each of the third and fourth attacks. Though the rising toll indicated that any protection offered by the foil strips would be temporary, even these losses were appreciably lower than those suffered in attacks on Hamburg before the use of Window.

In many respects, Hamburg was an ideal target even though it was

141

beyond Oboe range. The city lay on the Elbe River, so its brilliantly glowing image stood out against a dark background on H2S radar screens. Because it also lay close to the sea, the bombers had only a short flight over land-based enemy defenses before reaching the target.

Churchill praised Bomber Command's success over Hamburg, but what he wanted most of all was strikes on Berlin. He wanted Berliners to suffer as Londoners had suffered during the Blitz, and he had been pressing Harris since the fall of 1942 to attack the German capital in strength. Harris delayed. Earlier raids had cost more in bombers than they were worth in results. But by mid-November of 1943, Harris was ready to try it again. To wage what became known as the Battle of Berlin, he had a fleet of 948 combat-ready heavy bombers, which could carry enough explosives to make a raid on the city worth the effort. Moreover, bombing promised to be more accurate than ever, because H2S radar had been improved and was now carried by many bombers in the main force as well as by the Pathfinders.

The Pathfinders needed all the gadgets and cunning at their disposal, for the whole battle was fought, as Harris wrote in his memoirs, "in appalling weather and in conditions resembling those of no other campaign in the history of warfare." Few crews even caught a glimpse of Berlin. Some bombs fell as far as 30 miles from the city, but enough struck their targets to make the campaign a success. German records of the damage to Berlin are incomplete, but they show that after six raids 46 factories lay in ruins, an additional 259 were damaged and thousands of houses were wrecked. However, the damage inflicted on Berlin never reached the proportions of Hamburg's ruination, and industrial production in the capital city actually increased slightly under the ministrations of the assiduous Albert Speer.

Nevertheless, Goebbels admitted as early as November 25 that "conditions in the city are pretty hopeless." And shortly after the heaviest raid of all, on the night of February 15, Field Marshal Erhard Milch, Göring's deputy, told his staff: "Everyone should pay a visit to Berlin. It would then be realized that experiences such as we have undergone in the last few months cannot be endured indefinitely. That is impossible."

This precisely echoed Harris' often unpopular view that the bombing of cities would contribute more than any other strategic effort to the defeat of Germany. But such raids were costly. And neither Window nor diversionary raids seemed to substantially improve the odds for the bombers. From November 1943 to March 1944 Bomber Command lost 1,047 aircraft and crews.

The worst losses of any single bomber raid of the War occurred on the night of March 30, 1944. The target was Nuremberg, one of several cities struck as a diversionary tactic during the Battle of Berlin. The city lay deep in Germany, a flight of some 400 miles over occupied territory and German homeland. Defenses bristled along most of the route. Nuremberg, like Berlin, was well beyond the range of Oboe. Moreover, on H2S radar it looked just like other cities nearby. If the city was

A huge flare dropped by the RAF Pathfinder Force brilliantly illuminates an enemy aircraft-engine plant at Limoges, France, in 1944. Indispensable in night raids, Pathfinders swooped as low as 500 feet or less in their swift de Havilland Mosquitoes to mark targets for the heavy bombers.

Avro Lancasters of No. 57 Squadron bomb the Moderville steelworks, near Caen, in this 1944 painting by artist Michael Turner. To distinguish the target from surrounding structures, the Pathfinders have marked it with green flares.

obscured by clouds, the concentration of factories there that produced tanks and electrical equipment would, in all likelihood, suffer little damage in any bomber attack.

At 11:00 p.m., 795 bombers headed over the North Sea and across the Belgian coast for Nuremberg. The night air was clear en route to the target, not overcast as the weather report had promised. A bright half-moon illuminated the contrails of the bombers, pinpointing their positions for German night fighters. Bomber after bomber was shot down, many by planes armed with a 20-millimeter cannon that the Germans called *schräge Musik* (literally "slanted music," the German term for jazz) because it was unconventionally mounted to fire almost straight up. "We were attacked from immediately below," reported Flight Sergeant Guy Edwards, a gunner in the turret atop the fuselage of a No. 76 Squadron Halifax, "and it was obvious that we had encountered for the first time some form of aircraft that could fire vertically upwards with extreme accuracy because I saw the tracer in the cannon shells pass vertically upwards through all four engines and the wings." Flames fed by ruptured fuel tanks in the wings streamed along the Halifax's fuselage. Seconds later the bomber exploded. Edwards was blown clear and floated to safety on his parachute. The rest of the crew perished.

As the bombers flew on, clouds gathered over Nuremberg and the Pathfinders experienced insurmountable difficulties in marking the target. As Squadron Leader L. D. Leicester of No. 640 Squadron said later, "It was without a doubt the worst night that I can ever remember, and I could not recall when the RAF was thrown into so much confusion resulting, of course, in bombs being scattered anywhere."

Photoreconnaissance after the attack confirmed that little damage had been done to Nuremberg. One factory had been half destroyed; three others were merely inconvenienced. Most of the bombs had been strewn wildly across the countryside. But worse than the disappointing results was the cost. Of the nearly 800 bombers that set out for Germany, 95 never returned to England, a loss rate of 11.8 per cent.

By comparison, the raids on Berlin two months earlier suffered a substantially lower loss rate, only about 6.1 per cent—a figure that was just bearable to the men who ran the bombing offensive; it meant that planes and crews were being added to Bomber Command slightly faster than they were being shot down. The men who flew the missions, of course, were less sanguine. Many of them regarded a posting to Bomber Command operations as a terminal assignment. In 1943, Flight Lieutenant Denis Hornsey, a Halifax pilot in No. 76 Squadron, wrote in his unpublished memoirs: "If you live on the brink of death yourself, it is as if those who have gone have merely caught an earlier train to the same destination, and whatever that destination is, you will be sharing it soon, since you will almost certainly be catching the next one."

Hornsey survived the War, but thousands of others did not. A squadron's casualty rate could vary capriciously—none on one night, as many as half a dozen on another. Or, as in No. 76 Squadron, the losses could be fairly steady at the rate of one or two aircraft on each raid. Weeks sometimes passed without a single bomber crew completing its 30th operational sortie, the elusive ticket to six months in a rear-echelon job and safety.

The constant danger of their work strained the bravery of the air crews. Some of them jettisoned their bombloads well before reaching the target and returned to base. In other crews, nervous bombardiers, flinching at the flak bursting on every side, became "fringe merchants," releasing bombs several seconds early. To compensate, Pathfinders were sometimes instructed to drop their markers hundreds of yards beyond the aiming point.

Bomber crews that avoided confrontation with the enemy, however, risked official punishment at home. Greater than any other dread, for most men, was the fear of being LMF'd—grounded for "lack of moral fiber." Such a verdict was almost always a disgrace, and depending on the circumstances, it could result in a court-martial. Some men were sent to prison. Others were given a choice between a transfer to the Army and being booted out of the military altogether to dig coal.

Fearing heavier casualties, Harris resisted attempts by his superiors to dilute his area-bombing effort in favor of pinpoint targets. No man, however, wins all his battles. During the Ruhr campaign in the spring of 1943, the British Air Staff decided to knock out three important dams— the Möhne, the Eder and the Sorpe. The Möhne and Eder stored more than 346 million tons of water for the production of hydroelectric power. All three constituted the flood-control system for the Weser and Ruhr Rivers. These huge edifices were indestructible by ordinary bombs, but Barnes Wallis, designer of the Wellington bomber, had been working for many months perfecting a bomb that would do the job. The solution was not in the weapon's size—9,250 pounds—but in the fact that it was designed to sink into the water before exploding, so that its destructive power would be magnified by the so-called water-hammer effect of the shock waves moving through the incompressible fluid.

Harris, beset by "all sorts of enthusiasts and panacea-mongers," castigated the Wallis bomb as "just about the maddest proposition as a weapon we have yet come across." But in March 1943, persuaded by Air Chief Marshal Sir Charles Portal, Chief of the Air Staff, Harris relented and formed a new unit of Lancaster bombers, No. 617 Squadron, to drop the Wallis bombs. He recruited experienced crews who had already completed a full tour of operations, producing a *corps d'élite* with Wing Commander Guy Gibson appointed to command. A veteran of more than three years' combat experience, Gibson was a natural leader and the perfect choice to direct the attack on the dams.

To function correctly, the bombs had to be dropped from an altitude of no more than 60 feet. "At that height," wrote Gibson in 1944, "you would only have to hiccough and you would be in the drink." The plan called for each plane to carry one bomb and to skip it like a stone across the lake behind a dam. Upon striking the face of the dam, the bomb would sink 40 feet before it detonated and, it was fervently hoped, burst the dam. Gibson's men had only six short weeks to rehearse for the mission; the dams had to be bombed in the middle of May, when the water levels would be at their highest and the moon at its brightest.

Gibson led the attack on the night of May 16. The Lancasters headed first for the Möhne Dam. Despite a hail of ground fire from towers at each end of the structure, Gibson dropped his bomb perfectly; it skipped across the surface and sank next to the dam. But when the lake calmed after the shock of the explosion, Gibson could see that the dam was still intact. He then circled over the target and directed his squadronmates by radio as they made their attacks. The second bomber was set afire by the German defenders and its bomb overshot the dam. The next three aircraft all skipped their bombs precisely onto the target, and the last explosion opened a breach in the dam 100 yards wide.

"It was a most amazing sight," wrote Gibson. A wall of water 25 feet high surged down the valley, inundating or sweeping aside everything in its path, railways, bridges and automobiles. "I saw their headlights burning and I saw water overtake them and then the color of the headlights underneath the water changing from light blue to green, from green to dark purple, until there was no longer anything except the water bouncing down in great waves."

Gibson led the Lancasters that had not bombed the Möhne Dam to the next target, the Eder Dam. A few minutes later it gave way under the crushing blows of the exploding bombs. But the Sorpe Dam remained standing; destroying the first two targets had used up all the bombs. Of the 18 crews that started the raid, two failed to reach the target and eight were lost. Thirty-three members of the squadron were decorated and Gibson was awarded the Victoria Cross.

In August of 1943, Harris, who had been promoted to the rank of air chief marshal earlier that year, sent his bombers against another important pinpoint target—the rocket research center at Peenemünde on an island in the Baltic Sea, where the V-2 rocket with which

Water pours through a 300-foot-wide gap in the Möhne Dam, breached the day before in a bombing attack by nine Lancasters of No. 617 Squadron. Dubbed the Dam Busters after this success, the airmen of No. 617 were later called upon to attack the German battleship Tirpitz.

Hitler hoped to annihilate southern England was being developed.

Because the Peenemünde base consisted of three separate groups of buildings, it was estimated that an area attack would waste five bombs out of six. The solution was to bomb each group of buildings as a separate, distinct aiming point. But because the target was outside Oboe range and too dispersed for an attack by H2S, it would have to be bombed visually, by moonlight, from a comparatively low altitude.

Even under the brightest natural light, visual aiming would quickly deteriorate as smoke screens and smoke from fires blanketed the buildings, and this led to the appointment of a master bomber for the mission, a new role inspired by Guy Gibson's performance as an on-the-spot director of the dam-busting raid. The man chosen was 30-year-old Group Captain John Searby, formerly a flight commander in No. 106 Squadron. Socially aloof and shy, with a mocking smile, Searby had taken over No. 83 (Pathfinder) Squadron after two previous commanders had been shot down. His own vulnerability was emphasized by the appointment of two deputies to assume control should he share the fate of his predecessors.

Searby's task on August 17, 1943, was to watch the fall of the target markers dropped on Peenemünde by planes using H2S radar, correct the inevitable errors by giving instructions to the rest of the Pathfinders on the mission and broadcast to the approaching bomber stream which markers they should aim at and which they should ignore. Orbiting at 4,000 feet, halfway between the bombers and the ground, Searby was in constant danger from falling bombs as well as from enemy flak, but his calm, dispassionate voice guided the bombers and warned of scattered markers. The plan of attack called for each aiming point to receive 15 minutes of concentrated bombardment. A feint by other aircraft toward Berlin deceived German fighters for most of the mission, but during the last 15 minutes some 30 appeared. Of the 597 bombers that went to Peenemünde, 40 failed to return.

"My poor, poor Peenemünde," groaned the commandant, Major General Walter Dornberger, the next day. Temporarily at least, the rocket center had been knocked out. Seven or eight hundred men were killed, most of them slave workers from countries Hitler had conquered. Among the fatalities, however, were two key scientists—Walter Thiel, Germany's leading propulsion expert, and Chief Engineer Helmut Walther. Goebbels wrote in his diary that preparation of the V-2 was thrown back "four or even eight weeks," but the transfer of production to underground factories and the establishment of a new experimental base at Blinza, Poland, out of reach of Bomber Command, suggests that the raid disrupted Peenemünde operations more than Goebbels estimated.

The Germans did not abandon Peenemünde, despite the destruction there. Many of the facilities survived to nurture another terror weapon—the V-1 flying bomb. Spies in Europe had reported this new threat to the British, but the RAF's first glimpse of the 19-foot-long, stub-winged aircraft came from a reconnaissance photograph taken of Pee-nemünde on October 3, 1943. Another picture taken about eight weeks later revealed a V-1 on a launching ramp. This development was disturbing indeed. Dozens of such ramps, utterly mysterious until now, had been photographed in France, pointing directly at London.

Air raids on the launch sites began immediately. The British and Americans sent fighter-bombers at low level and heavy bombers at high level. But the best results were those obtained by speedy RAF Mosquito light bombers. Built primarily of wood, the de Havilland Mosquito could take a great deal of punishment and survive to fly again. Following its introduction in 1941, it had rapidly become an RAF workhorse. It replaced other bombers as the primary Pathfinder aircraft. Coastal Command used it for reconnaissance and to attack ships at sea. In Fighter Command, it saw intruder duty, following German planes to their bases and shooting them down as they attempted to land. Bomber Command employed Mosquitoes as low-level attack bombers, and nowhere with better results than against the V-1 launching sites in France.

By the end of December, 52 V-1 launch sites had been cratered with bombs. New ramps were continually being exposed by reconnaissance, and another 79 were hit in the first half of January 1944. "If Allied bombing continues at the present rate for two more weeks," said Colonel Max Wachtel, head of the experimental unit entrusted with launching V-1s, "the hope of ever using the original site system operationally will have to be abandoned." Abandoned it duly was, in favor of temporary sites. The bombers sought them out as eagerly as the permanent ones, but it was impossible to destroy them all.

Pinpoint attacks, like the raids on V-1 launch sites, Peenemünde and the dams in the Ruhr, though successful in many respects, were merely a sideshow to the strategic bombing that aimed to destroy Germany's capacity for war. Between March 1943 and April 1944, Bomber Command flew 74,900 sorties and dropped 200,333 tons of bombs on German cities. More than 2,800 bombers were shot down.

RAF Bomber Command and the American Eighth Air Force, which was now flying regular daytime raids over Germany, bit into German war production. For example, Speer estimated that, because of Allied bombing, aircraft factories were producing only half the number of fighters that would have been possible otherwise. But perhaps more important was the fact that the offensive had helped to relieve German pressure on the Soviet Union. Some one and a half million Germans, many of them men who might have served in ground forces on the Eastern Front, were instead engaged in the work of air defense and repairing bomb damage. Moreover, strategic bombing forced Göring to transfer fighters from the Eastern Front, where they could ill be spared, to France and Germany. In addition, he continued to siphon Luftwaffe strength from the Mediterranean to a point where the German air arm's influence there became minimal. Above all, Harris' Bomber Command and Major General Ira Eaker's United States Eighth Air Force compelled

"Beyond praise": a gallery of Royal Air Force heroes

"For tenacity and devotion to duty beyond praise," read the citation that accompanied the Victoria Cross awarded to bomber pilot William Reid, whose picture and story appear on page 151. The same ringing words could be applied to all the RAF pilot heroes presented on this and the following pages. Some, such as the flamboyant Cobber Kain *(below)*, who flew a Hurricane in France in 1939 and the spring of 1940, gained their fame early in World War II. Other fliers, including Guy Gibson and Leonard Cheshire *(page 152)*, earned recognition as they carried the air war to German skies in the conflict's later years.

Not all won the Victoria Cross; that supreme award was the near monopoly of bomber crews, who had all-too-frequent opportunities for heroism as they flew sortie after sortie through bursting flak and swarming German night fighters. Their chances of surviving a string of missions were poor; they faced, their chief, Air Marshal Sir Arthur Harris, said, "the virtual certainty of death, probably in one of its least pleasant forms." But the fighter pilots, too, courted extinction on every sortie and also faced it with a determination, courage and flying skill that were "beyond praise" and sometimes beyond imagining.

The men included here are not, for the most part, identified by rank. Such outstanding pilots—or those who lived long enough—were rapidly promoted and thus held several ranks as their careers, and the War, progressed.

EDGAR JAMES "COBBER" KAIN

This pilot (the nickname meant "friend" in the slang of his native New Zealand) became the RAF's first fighter ace of the War after his squadron was sent to France in the fall of 1939. An aggressive, slashing attacker, Kain sailed into the large swarms of Luftwaffe planes that supported the German blitzkrieg of May and June 1940 and led all RAF pilots during that early stage of the War with a record of 17 enemy aircraft shot down. He was killed when, with customary exuberance, he buzzed his own airfield, flew too low and crashed.

ADOLPH GYSBERT "SAILOR" MALAN

To many of his fellow pilots, Malan—who shot down the first two of his total of 32 enemy planes on his very first mission over Dunkirk in May 1940—was the supreme master of fighter tactics and the greatest flying leader in the RAF.

He wrote 10 cardinal rules of aerial combat for the crack No. 74 Squadron, which he commanded throughout the Battle of Britain. These cogent maxims (sample: "Always turn and face the attack") were soon the bible on every fighter base. He was a dead shot and above all he had what his fellow ace and squadronmate Mungo Park called "cold courage." Malan was so calm during combat that he once methodically replaced a small electric bulb in his Spitfire's reflector sight while in the middle of a dogfight.

Born in South Africa in 1910, Malan was called Sailor because he had spent five years in the British merchant navy before joining the RAF in 1935. He was 30 years of age during the Battle of Britain, old for a fighter pilot, but his maturity gave his leadership a firm authority. He was promoted to wing commander and led his fighters on sweeps over France in 1943 and 1944. After the War he returned to his native South Africa, where he became a successful sheep rancher.

JAMES HARRY "GINGER" LACEY

The red-haired, freckled Lacey was the top-scoring noncommissioned pilot (he was a sergeant) of the Battle of Britain, with 15 kills. He was in constant action during the crucial summer of 1940, at times flying seven or eight sorties a day. For his "consistent efficiency and great courage," as one citation read, he was awarded the Distinguished Flying Medal twice and given a commission.

Lacey later flew fighter sweeps over France and then served as a squadron leader in Burma. His final tally of enemy aircraft was 28.

MARMADUKE THOMAS ST. JOHN "PAT" PATTLE

Although little-known to the public because he flew in out-of-the-way theaters of war, South African-born Pat Pattle was probably the top-scoring RAF ace. In North Africa and Greece he racked up an official score of 23 enemy planes. His squadronmates insisted, however, that Pattle, a superb pilot and marksman, shot down at least 20 more during the last days of the Greek fighting. Precisely how many is not known, since the records detailing these later kills were lost when the British evacuated Greece.

He was certainly the most successful pilot to fly the outdated Gladiator biplane; in it he achieved all of his official victories. After his squadron was re-equipped with Hurricanes, his wingmen saw him on one occasion shoot down an entire three-plane patrol and on another destroy five adversaries in a single day during which he flew five missions.

Ignoring the fatigue of five-sortie days, Pattle continued to fly until April 22, 1941, when, after he had downed three German fighters, his Hurricane was riddled by two Me 110s and fell straight into the Aegean Sea.

JAMES EDGAR "JOHNNY" JOHNSON

The RAF's official top scorer, with 38 confirmed kills to his credit, English-born Johnny Johnson set two other notable records: All of his aerial victories were over enemy fighters, more elusive prey than bombers, and in a marathon 515 combat missions his Spitfire was holed only once by enemy bullets.

All of Johnson's missions were offensive fighter sweeps or bomber-escort flights over Europe. He rose to command an entire fighter wing, survived the War and stayed in the peacetime RAF.

WILLIAM "BILL" REID

A Scot from Glasgow, Bill Reid won the Victoria Cross for one of the most heroic performances of the War. His Lancaster had just crossed the Dutch coast on the night of November 3, 1943, when a shell from a German fighter blasted away the cockpit windshield, the shell fragments wounding Reid in several places.

Ignoring his injuries and the gale blowing through his unprotected cockpit, he continued into Germany toward the target, Düsseldorf. Soon his Lancaster was raked by fire from another fighter, which killed or wounded most of the crew and hit Reid again. Still he flew on, although so weak from loss of blood that he was forced to lock his arms around the control column to keep the plane in level flight. Reid finally reached Düsseldorf, dropped his bombs and then flew his battered aircraft back to England.

Recovered from his wounds, he continued to fly bomber missions until July 31, 1944, when his plane was nearly cut in half by a misdirected bomb from a British aircraft flying above him. Reid bailed out but spent the last 10 months of the War in a German prison camp.

ALAN CHRISTOPHER "AL" DEERE

A gifted pilot who shot down three Me 109s on his first day of combat in 1940, New Zealander Al Deere was also the RAF's survival expert, with nine crash landings or bailouts. The first occurred when Deere, his Spitfire damaged over Dunkirk, crash-landed in Belgium, made his way to Dunkirk by bus, bicycle and on foot, and was evacuated by ship.

Later, during the Battle of Britain, he collided with an Me 109 but somehow landed in an open field and leaped free of the blazing wreckage. He survived the War with 21 confirmed kills.

DOUGLAS ROBERT STEUART BADER

Bader, an Englishman who had lost both legs in a prewar crash and flew with metal ones, was a fiery leader and a cool air tactician with 22 kills. During the Battle of Britain his squadron of Canadians downed 63 enemy planes while losing only three pilots, a ratio of 20 to 1 unapproached by any other RAF squadron.

Later he led a wing on sweeps over France. A collision forced him to parachute into enemy territory in August 1941, and he spent the rest of the War in German prison camps.

GEOFFREY LEONARD CHESHIRE

Cheshire, who grew up in the quiet neighborhood of Oxford University, the son of a professor, did more than any other pilot to turn the violent art of bombing into a science. He pioneered precise low-level target marking at night, first in heavy four-engined Lancasters and later in swift, fragile Mosquito bombers. In a Mosquito he would dive to within 200 feet of a factory roof to be sure his flares pinpointed the target for the following streams of bombers.

Cheshire flew perilous bomber missions over Germany and occupied Europe between 1940 and 1944, surviving more than three normal tours of duty and 100 combat missions. He was awarded the Victoria Cross not for a single valorous act but for his unparalleled four-year demonstration of stamina, courage and skill.

GUY PENROSE GIBSON

Guy Gibson began flying combat missions on the first day of the War and in about a year completed a bomber pilot's normal first tour of 30 missions.

Posted to a training unit, he refused such tame duty and flew 99 sorties as a night-fighter pilot. Again sent to a flight-training school, Gibson again objected and did a second tour in bombers. He was then asked to lead the elite No. 617 Squadron on the famous Dam Busters raid that shattered two German dams, for which he won the Victoria Cross.

Grounded again, Gibson volunteered for one last mission, leading a night raid over Germany in September, 1944. After marking the target and watching the bombs fall, he radioed his crews, "Nice work chaps, now beat it home." It was Gibson's last message; his plane was shot down during the return flight. "He lived to see the dawn of certain victory," wrote Air Marshal Harris, "and no man did more to bring it about."

the Luftwaffe to emphasize the production of fighters in preference to bombers. Forced into this defensive role, the German air force could do little to hinder preparations by the Allies for an invasion of Europe.

Plans for just such an invasion, code-named *Overlord,* brought Bomber Command's attacks against German cities to a temporary halt. Harris was ordered instead to attack railroad marshaling yards in France. Destruction of such rail centers would slow to a fatal crawl the German Army's ability to concentrate forces against the planned Allied bridgehead in Normandy.

The Transportation Plan, as it was called, met powerful opposition from three sources. Harris, doubting the ability of his crews to achieve the bombing precision necessary to wreck railroads, believed that the strongest support that his command could give to *Overlord* would be to intensify the attack on German industrial centers. To relax this offensive would be to undo all the work of the past nine months and allow German industry to recover. Churchill feared that bombing rail yards would cost the lives of too many French civilians—more than 40,000 of them by one estimate. Major General Carl Spaatz, who was in overall command of the United States Strategic Air Forces in Europe, preferred to batter Germany's oil facilities. But Field Marshal Bernard Montgomery, who was to command *Overlord* ground forces in Normandy, prevailed. He regarded the crippling of enemy military movement toward what would surely be a tenuous Allied foothold in France during the three weeks after D-Day as critical to the operation's success. So the heavy bombers were sent in.

Several missions had already been flown by April 15, when a complete list of targets for the Transportation Plan was issued by Air Chief Marshal Tedder. Of the 79 rail yards to be destroyed 37 were allocated to Bomber Command and 42 to Americans and to other British units. Between the beginning of April and the end of June, Bomber Command flew more than 13,000 sorties against rail targets. To Harris' surprise, the Pathfinders had become so adept at marking targets that all of the objectives assigned to Bomber Command were pulverized and no return visits were necessary. Of the remaining 42 targets, 38 were judged to have been equally devastated. "The French railway system is in complete chaos," admitted Radio Paris, a German-controlled French station, in a broadcast on May 23 that also castigated the British for the civilian casualties caused by the bombing.

RAF Bomber Command and the United States Eighth Air Force were only one facet of the air power brought to bear against the enemy in anticipation of *Overlord.* The entire Allied tactical air arm had been reorganized for the occasion into the Allied Expeditionary Air Force (AEAF) under the overall command of Air Marshal Sir Trafford Leigh-Mallory. Among its components was the Second Tactical Air Force (2nd TAF), an all-British outfit led by Air Marshal Sir Arthur Coningham and made up of two fighter groups from RAF Fighter Command (the rest of Fighter Command was redesignated the Air Defence of Great Britain).

Other British units in the AEAF were the No. 2 (Light Bomber) Group, detached from Bomber Command, and a reconnaissance wing. The United States contributed the Ninth Air Force. Coastal Command remained essentially unchanged. Its mission: to sink as many German ships as could be found and to protect the vast D-Day armada as it steamed toward France. In overall control of these air components was General Dwight Eisenhower, commander of all Allied forces.

As D-Day neared, Typhoons and Spitfires of the 2nd TAF repeatedly strafed the German coastal radar system, erected to detect approaching ships, and struck at German coastal batteries. On the night before the invasion, 1,130 aircraft from Bomber Command bombarded 10 batteries overlooking the landing area; only one of them opened fire the next day. Allied aircraft—bombers, fighters and fighter-bombers—also blasted bridges and hammered at German airfields. But for every target in or near the proposed bridgehead area on the Cherbourg peninsula, the Allies struck two located in other areas in order to mislead the enemy about the site of the landings.

As the Allied planners had foreseen, the decisive element on D-Day was overwhelming air power. General Eisenhower had more than 8,000 planes at his disposal, and on the night of June 5th and on D-Day, June 6th, they flew 14,700 sorties. By dawn, the bombers had stunned the defenders into a stupor and an umbrella of fighters protected the beaches. "Without your strategic bombing of our lines of communica-

This cratered landscape in Normandy shows the effects of the carpet bombing by RAF support aircraft that preceded the invading Allied armies in June of 1944. By laying a dense carpet of bombs on German-held territory, the British bombers were able to weaken enemy resistance to the advancing ground forces.

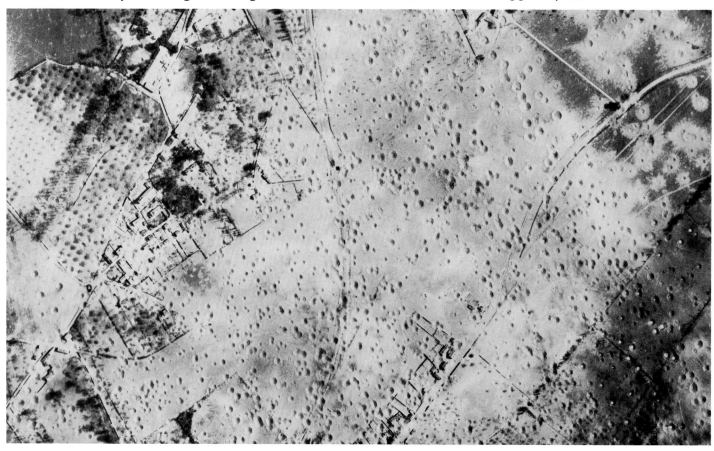

tion," lamented one German officer, "without your gigantic aerial coverage of the landings, your invasion ships and barges would have been sunk or driven out to sea."

As soon as a foothold was established on the Continent, fighters of the 2nd TAF began operating from hastily constructed airfields in France. One field was so near the front line that the Typhoons based there found themselves diving across their own runway to discharge their rockets and cannon into enemy concentrations only 1,000 yards beyond. From takeoff to landing, a mission could last less than 10 minutes. Aircraft were in such abundant supply that ground units were able to call on their help at will. Air Marshal Coningham introduced a ground-support system he had evolved in Italy, called the cab rank: Fighter-bombers kept station in flying lines overhead until they were summoned by controllers in forward tanks or armored cars to strike at enemy positions holding up the Allied ground advance. Mosquitoes and Mustangs ranged far and wide on armed reconnaissance missions, attacking trains and convoys day and night. A French farmer saw German soldiers flee from a road when attacked by the RAF. "They plunged into the doorways of houses, into cowsheds and barns—anywhere to escape the eyes of the pilots. In order to leave their vehicles as quickly as possible the German soldiers had removed the doors, and one of their number always lay on one of the front mudguards looking upwards and scanning the sky."

After devastating a column of German panzers, RAF Typhoons pull up out of the attack to return to their base in this contemporary painting. These heavily armed fighter-bombers were used extensively in the Normandy invasion. "We could do nothing against them," said one panzer division commander.

Low-level attacks by Typhoons, in particular, proved stupefying. "They came down in hundreds," said General von Luttwitz, commanding the 2nd Panzer Division, "firing their rockets at the concentrated tanks and vehicles. We could do nothing against them." One German armored thrust, said General Hans Speidel, was "completely wrecked exclusively by the Allied air forces." On June 11, Field Marshal Rommel, who months before had been sent from Africa to defend France, reported to Field Marshal Keitel in Berlin: "The enemy has complete control over the battle area and up to 100 kilometers behind the front."

The situation was just as grim offshore. Wherever German shipping plied the European coastline, Coastal Command was likely to strike. In mid-June the Germans attempted to convoy two new vessels—an 8,000-ton merchantman and a 4,000-ton torpedo-boat tender—from the shipyards in Rotterdam to the Baltic Sea to complete their fitting out. The convoy was an attractive target—and a dangerous one: Its 19 ships could put up enough flak to counter almost any attack.

Coastal Command struck the ships off the Dutch island of Schiermonnikoog. Flying in line-abreast formation, 32 Beaufighters, cannon and rockets blazing, dived on the convoy, diverting the ships' fire from 10 additional Beaufighters that raced in at low level with torpedoes. The two new ships were left sinking rapidly by the stern. One escort vessel blew up, and five others were set on fire. Of the 42 Beaufighters involved, five suffered superficial flak damage, but none was lost and not a single crew member was injured.

U-boats, seeking to prey on *Overlord* convoys, were out in force. In the first four days after D-Day, 25 of them were discovered and attacked by Coastal Command aircraft off the coast of France; six were sunk. From then on the U-boats lurked at periscope depth, where they proved more elusive but, because of their lower speed underwater, also less menacing to the Allied resupply of *Overlord*. In the North Atlantic, however, U-boat crews showed all their old fighting spirit and stayed on the surface to slug it out with Coastal Command's flying boats.

After nightfall on July 17, 1944, a Coastal Command crew in an American-built Consolidated Catalina flying boat, patrolling 700 miles from its base at Sullom Voe in the Shetland Islands, picked up an unidentified vessel on radar, five miles ahead. The pilot, Flight Lieutenant John Cruickshank, climbed from his 200-foot search altitude into some scattered clouds to steal up on the ship. A minute later, Cruickshank saw it—a German submarine. The U-boat immediately opened fire with its 20- and 37-millimeter antiaircraft cannon.

Cruickshank circled once and headed for the German sub, but his depth charges failed to release. On the second try, an antiaircraft shell exploded inside the plane, killing the navigator instantly and riddling three other men, including Cruickshank, with shrapnel. Ignoring his wounds, the pilot pressed his attack and dropped his depth charges perfectly. The water-hammer effect of the explosions shattered the submarine's hull, and the *U-347* sank beneath the waves.

Buzzing over the Bay of Biscay, Royal Air Force Coastal Command Mosquitoes assault enemy shipping shortly after the June 1944 invasion of Normandy. By mid-August Coastal Command had routed German U-boats from their ports along the bay and sunk many as they fled to Norway.

The Catalina was more than five hours from home, with gasoline streaming from a punctured fuel line. Even if the fuel held out, a gaping hole below the aircraft's water line made it likely that the flying boat would sink on landing. Cruickshank had lost too much blood to continue flying the Catalina, so his copilot, Flight Sergeant Jack Garnett, took over and Cruickshank lay down in a bunk normally used for resting during long missions. He refused morphine, afraid that it might dull his thinking along with the pain.

As they approached the flying boat base at Sullom Voe, Cruickshank insisted on being helped into the copilot's seat to direct Garnett in the landing. As soon as the plane touched down, water rushed into the hull, and Cruickshank and Garnett were able to save the craft only by gunning the engines and taxiing it onto the beach.

Medics later counted 72 wounds in Cruickshank's legs and chest. He recovered and for his bravery under fire was awarded the Victoria Cross, one of four awarded to Coastal Command pilots during the War (all the rest were bestowed posthumously). Garnett won a Distinguished Flying Medal.

Bomber Command, meanwhile, flew sortie after sortie against the German rear, crippling enemy movement by interdicting roads and railroads. Harris' heavies even played a tactical role, laying carpets of bombs on enemy concentrations that had stalled advancing ground forces. Such assistance was made possible only by low-level target-marking techniques pioneered by Wing Commander Leonard Cheshire, who after Guy Gibson commanded No. 617 Squadron of dam-busting fame. It was thought that these methods would reduce to an acceptable level the risk of bombs straying into friendly troops.

The largest of these attacks occurred at Caen in July. Stiff German resistance had prevented Field Marshal Montgomery's British and Canadian divisions from capturing the city, the key to German defenses in Normandy. On the 7th of July, 457 RAF four-engined bombers delivered 2,363 tons of bombs on Germans who were dug in north of Caen. German resistance faltered and Allied troops surged into the city by the afternoon of the next day. But their momentum was not sufficient to capture it; the enemy had regrouped to make another stand.

For 10 days, the impasse continued. Then on July 18 another air raid, far larger than the first, battered Colombelles, a suburb of Caen where German resistance was centered. In this joint British-American effort, 1,919 heavy and medium bombers dropped 7,700 tons of explosives on the Germans. With remarkable resilience, the Germans bounced back from the bombing with enough resolve to prevent Montgomery's forces from breaking through. Caen was finally cleared of Germans on July 20 at a cost of more than 5,000 men. Although the raids had not obliterated the German defenses, they were enough to convince General von Kluge, the commander of all German ground forces in Normandy, that it would be impossible to win the war on the ground in the face of the enemy's complete command of the air. He wrote to Hitler on July 21 that he could see no way to counter the ''annihilating effect'' of Allied bombers except to ''withdraw from the battlefield.''

Paradoxically, this use of heavy bombers posed problems for the Allies themselves. Cities reduced in this fashion became a jumble of rubble. Foot soldiers could scramble through the blocked streets, but tanks, essential to a successful ground assault, were often rendered useless by piles of debris. Moreover, in spite of a high degree of accuracy, the bombing could go awry as it did on July 25, about 40 miles west of Caen. American bombs aimed at a German tank division fell short, killing or wounding hundreds of American troops. After this incident General Eisenhower, at first enthusiastic about close support of infantry by heavy bombers, forbade further use of such aircraft in this role.

As the invasion progressed, an old threat reappeared. On June 13 the Germans, having by then built enough temporary V-1 sites to mount a large-scale attack, began to launch flying bombs against England. The makeshift launching pads had replaced the battered permanent sites, and as soon as one was destroyed another emerged. By September, Bomber Command had aimed 60,000 tons of bombs at these sites. Yet the Germans still were able to send thousands of the terror weapons buzzing toward London.

When the flying bombs reached England, they faced a gauntlet of antiaircraft batteries and patrolling fighters of the Air Defence of Great

Britain. The V-1 was a formidable challenge to a fighter pilot. It usually flew slightly faster than his aircraft, so a stern chase was generally futile. The best tactic was to lie in wait at a higher altitude, then dive on the bomb as it sped past. But the V-1 was small and thus difficult to hit with gunfire—especially at ranges greater than 100 yards, the distance considered essential for safety: A bomb that exploded in mid-air usually wrecked a fighter that ventured closer.

Among the few aircraft that could overtake a V-1 was the Spitfire Mark XIV with a top speed of more than 400 miles per hour. And occasionally, when a pilot ran out of ammunition, he resorted to a daring tactic intended to make the robot weapon lose its flight stability by toppling the gyroscopes of its guidance system. "I placed my starboard wing-tip under the port wing of the bomb," wrote Paul Leva, a Belgian who flew for the RAF, "came up slowly, made contact as softly as I could, and then moved the stick violently back and to the left." The Spitfire went into a steep climbing turn and Leva momentarily lost sight of the bomb. Then he saw it going down steeply, "hitting the ground and exploding with a blinding crash."

The same technique brought the first combat victory to the only Allied jet fighter to serve in the War—the RAF's Gloster Meteor. On August 4, 1944, Flying Officer T. D. Dean of No. 616 Squadron attacked a V-1 over the English coast, but his guns jammed. So, speeding along at more than 400 miles per hour, Dean edged the end of his Meteor's wing under that of the buzz bomb and tipped the V-1 into a fatal dive.

At about the same time that Flying Officer Dean capsized his V-1 over England, it was becoming clear in France that the Germans lacked the strength to push the Allies out of Normandy. *Overlord* had succeeded. And it had done so in large measure because the Allied air forces had achieved their goals of immobilizing the enemy in a wasteland of useless roads and railroads, denying him air support from the Luftwaffe, and battering him with constant air attacks. In helping the armies to drive the Germans from France and the Low Countries, the Allied air forces also garnered a strategic advantage. The Germans had been forced to abandon territory from which they had operated their air-raid early-warning system, a network that had accounted for the loss of hundreds of RAF aircraft. To the leaders of Bomber Command, with a force that now numbered 1,100 heavy bombers, it seemed that the opportunity for a final and overwhelming strategic offensive, in conjunction with the Americans, was at hand.

The Allied leaders agreed that oil was to be the primary target, followed by transportation—roads, railroads, canals. By October 1944 the offensive was in full swing. In that month alone Bomber Command directed nearly 17,000 sorties at Germany. But although the bombers damaged many oil installations, only 6 per cent of the sorties were aimed at petroleum facilities; the rest were targeted against cities. Suspecting Harris of trying to fight the War his own way, Sir Charles Portal, who had been elevated to the rank of marshal of the RAF, rebuked the Bomber Command leader in a letter and issued a directive in November stressing the agreed priorities.

Harris responded by turning a far greater proportion of his command's effort against oil. By February 1945, Bomber Command had deposited 62,339 tons of ordnance on petroleum targets in waves of attacks that, according to Speer, caused "shattering damage." The United States Eighth Air Force had dropped a roughly equal tonnage on petroleum installations. Germany's flow of fuel slowed to a trickle.

Yet it was disruption of transportation that became the greatest single cause of the decline in Germany's industrial production. Damage to the Ruhr's rail and canal networks, for example, choked coal deliveries to such a degree that steel production plummeted to less than half the minimum tonnage required to keep industry going. "It is transport that governs all," said Speer.

A Lancaster of No. 617 Squadron releases its Tallboy over the Tirpitz in this painting of the November 1944 raid.

Not daring to take victory for granted, Harris' crews stepped up their attacks on German industry, mounting 26 major assaults in the first four months of 1945. After January 1945, Germany's gas and water systems, its railroads and its means of producing electricity had been reduced to an unworkable jumble. Many major cities had been bombed until further raids were pointless, and the few untouched cities were of little military significance. Yet the raids continued, reflecting Harris' conviction "that bombing anything in Germany is better than bombing nothing." It is little wonder, then, that Harris raised only the mildest objection when he was ordered to bomb the city of Dresden. In his opinion, the city was one of the few that was not worth attacking.

Dresden was a pearl, the site of some of the finest examples of 17th Century Baroque architecture in Europe. It was also a rail center and the hub of the telephone and telegraph systems in eastern Germany. In the suburbs, smatterings of light industry manufactured optics, radar components and fuses for shells fired by the German Navy's antiaircraft guns. But by early 1945, Germany was too near defeat for these industries to make a difference. Moreover, an attack would endanger about 26,000 Allied prisoners of war who were being held in the city and forced to work in the post office, the railroad yards and elsewhere. Also Dresden had become swollen with refugees driven west by the Soviet final thrust into eastern Germany, which began on October 16, 1944.

It was a decision by the Allied Joint Chiefs of Staff to support this Soviet push westward that sealed the fate of Dresden. By laying the city in ruins, the Allies sought to lower the morale of the Germans and stir up such confusion behind their front lines that effective resistance to the Soviets would collapse in disarray. Harris' objection was overruled, and Dresden became business as usual for the bombers.

In the space of about 14 hours—beginning at 10:15 p.m. on February 13, 1945—773 Lancasters of RAF Bomber Command and 450 B-17 Flying Fortresses of the United States Eighth Air Force dumped nearly 3,500 tons of high-explosive and incendiary bombs on the center of Dresden. The first wave of British bombers set the city ablaze. By the time the second wave of bombers arrived three hours later, Dresden was an inferno. "The fantastic glow from 200 miles away," wrote one pilot, "grew ever brighter as we moved into the target. At 20,000 feet we could see details in the unearthly blaze that had never been visible before; for the first time in many operations I felt sorry for the population below." The third wave of bombers—American B-17s—seemed superfluous.

The fire storm that developed in Dresden was even more devastating than the one that had ravaged Hamburg 19 months earlier. As the flames spread and intensified, an enormous volume of superheated gases billowed into the sky. The surrounding air mass that poured in to fill the void created by this updraft caused hurricane-force winds that howled through the city, feeding the fire and sweeping people into the heart of the conflagration. The fire storm lasted only a few hours, but

A big bomb for a big job

Commissioned in 1941, the German Navy's mighty 42,500-ton *Tirpitz* was a grave threat to Allied shipping. Though British planes attacked the *Tirpitz* repeatedly, they had little effect on the battleship's double layer of armor plate until 1944, when British inventor Sir Barnes Wallis built a special bomb for the job.

It was the Tallboy, a 12,030-pound monster capable of piercing the *Tirpitz'* tough hide. Soon, two squadrons of RAF bombers—cruising at treetop level when over enemy territory to avoid German radar—flew to the Soviet Union to stage a surprise attack on the battleship in Norway's Alten Fjord.

Using mountains to shield their approach from enemy radar, 27 Lancasters attacked the *Tirpitz* from the southeast on September 15, 1944. As the bombers swooped in, the ship's smoke generators hurriedly belched forth a dense, obscuring cloud. The planes scored only one direct hit, but one Tallboy was enough to render the *Tirpitz* unseaworthy. Planning to use her for stationary coastal defense, the Germans moved her south to Tromso, Norway. There, on November 12, thirty Lancasters flying out of Scotland set upon her and sank her.

Fire-bombed by the RAF on January 7, 1945, a stricken Munich illumines the night with flames that signal defeat for Germany.

Dresden continued to burn for seven days and eight nights. Thousands upon thousands of inhabitants were trapped in cellars beneath their burning homes. Refugees, seeking shelter in the bowels of the railroad station, suffocated. "Never would I have thought," said Hanns Voigt, a German official in charge of identifying the dead, "that death could come to so many people in so many different ways. Never had I expected to see people interred in that state: burnt, cremated, torn and crushed to death; there were wretched refugees from the east clad only in rags, and people from the opera in all their finery. Across the city, along the streets wafted the unmistakable stench of decaying flesh." By Voigt's estimate, 135,000 people perished; some postwar analysts put the figure at 25,000 dead.

The Dresden raids were part of a larger plan, Operation *Thunderclap,* designed to wreak havoc on other German cities, including Berlin. The object was to induce the enemy to surrender sooner. But the destruction at Dresden so staggered Churchill that he killed the operation. "Otherwise," he said, "we shall come into control of an utterly ruined land." And indeed, by early April of 1945 there were no more strategic targets in Germany worth hitting anyway. Nearly every major German city— Berlin, Hamburg, Munich, Stuttgart and Frankfurt—plus a host of smaller ones had been heavily damaged by Allied bombers. Harris' force was assigned to drop bombs in support of tactical operations on the ground and to drop food to the starving populace of Holland.

Harris' heavies flew their last combat sorties on May 2, 1945. Six days later the Third Reich surrendered, and the crews and aircraft of Bomber Command, so recently instruments of the apocalypse, turned to the rewarding task of repatriating prisoners of war to England. "The most touching part of each trip," remembered one crewman, "was when the white cliffs of Dover came in sight. Then as many chaps as possible would crowd into the navigator's and engineer's cockpit and peer out with eager eyes."

For the RAF in Europe, the spring of 1945 was indeed a time of flowers in gun barrels. Halfway around the world, on the other hand, the bloody fray continued *(pages 164-171),* as the Japanese persisted in a contest that they had no hope of winning.

But after the last bullet was fired and the final bomb dropped, when the contributions were tallied up, it would be clear that the Royal Air Force had played an indispensable role in the War. In the Battle of Britain, in the Battle of the Atlantic, in the Bomber offensive, in overseas theaters and in the invasion of Europe, British fliers helped immeasurably to shorten the War and saved countless lives in doing so. In this huge contribution to ultimate victory, all the RAF commands shared in proportion. But the costs struck disproportionately. Of the 70,253 RAF fliers killed in the War, 55,573 were in Bomber Command. "There is no parallel in warfare," wrote Harris, "to such courage and determination in the face of danger over so prolonged a period." ︎〜〜

The road back to Burma

After more than five years of monumental conflict, the war in Europe at last drew to a close in the spring of 1945. But while the RAF pilots and crews in England and on the Continent were celebrating their part in the victory over Germany, their comrades in the Far East were still locked in a fierce struggle with the tenacious Japanese.

In March, Lieutenant General Sir William Slim's British Fourteenth Army, marching south from India, took Mandalay in central Burma and thus opened the way to Rangoon and the eventual Allied liberation of all Southeast Asia. In an order of the day congratulating his troops, Slim paid special tribute to the men of the RAF: "They never failed us," he said, "and it is their victory as much as ours."

Indeed, the British return to Burma would scarcely have been possible but for the combined might of British and American air power. Newly equipped with American-built B-24 Liberator heavy bombers, the RAF crippled the enemy's life lines by attacking bridges and trains along some 5,000 miles of Japanese-controlled railroads and by destroying enemy cargo ships.

Now, as the army prepared for the final drive to Rangoon, the bombers ranged ahead to pound the city's port and supply dumps while RAF fighters blasted the enemy's forward airfields in order to clear the way for the transport squadrons that would supply Slim's men on the march. In order to take Rangoon before the monsoon began in May, the Allies decided to mount a dual airborne and amphibious assault on the city.

On May 1 two squadrons of C-47 Dakota transport planes dropped a battalion of paratroops, Gurkhas flown from British India, on the outskirts of Rangoon. At the same time, six convoys of troopships protected by RAF and Fleet Air Arm fighters were approaching the Burmese capital by sea. But before they could reach their goal the next day, an RAF Mosquito flew low over the city and discovered that the Japanese had fled. Thus on May 3, 1945, more than three years after the British retreat from Burma, Rangoon was reoccupied without a fight.

A dense cloud of smoke rises above a Japanese supply dump at Yenangyaung in central Burma during an attack by Royal Air Force Liberators in February of 1945.

An exploding bomb sends a massive column of water rising into the air as the RAF attacks a bridge on the Bangkok-Singapore railway. To reach such targets the Liberators flew as far as 2,000 miles from their bases near Calcutta in India.

Casting its giant, ominous shadow on the target, a low-flying RAF Liberator drops four high-explosive bombs on a wooden road bridge in Lower Burma. The attack was part of a systematic campaign to reduce the enemy's transport to chaos.

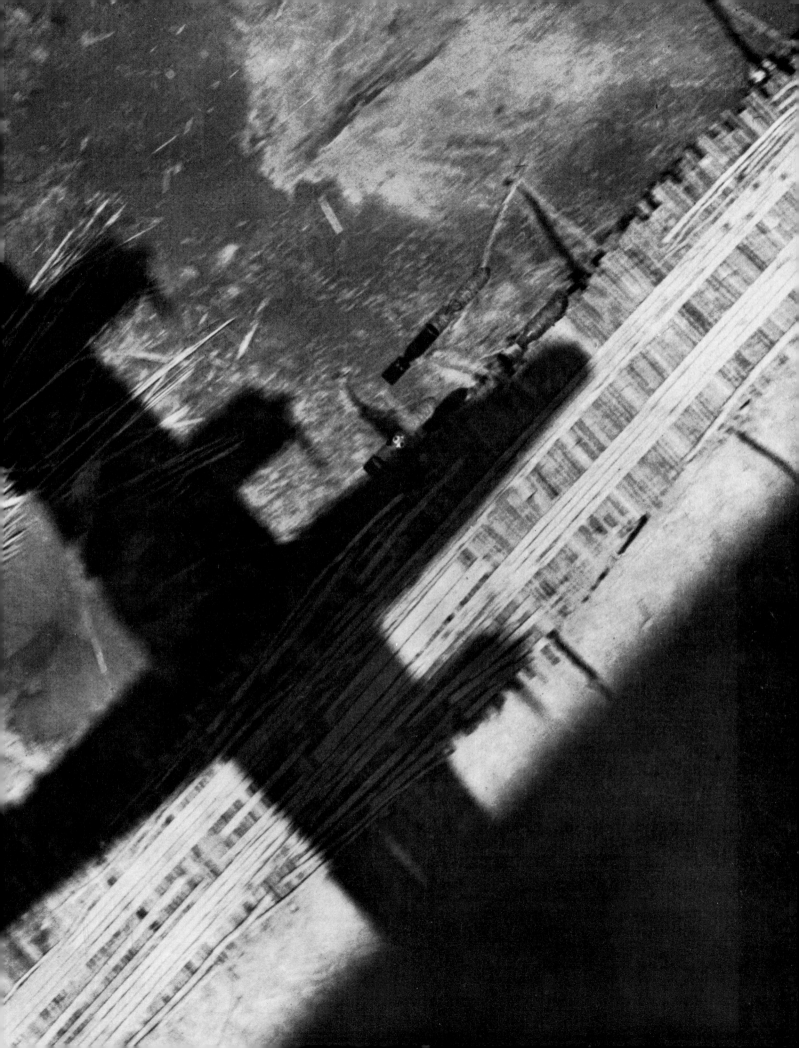

Gurkha paratroopers drop to earth at Elephant Point outside Rangoon to begin the final Allied move into the Burmese capital.

Rangoon's dock area is a field of rubble after RAF air strikes that preceded the city's capture in 1945. The Japanese had stored enough supplies to last six months at the docks and in some 1,700 dumps that were hidden in and around the city.

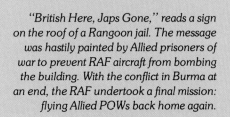

"British Here, Japs Gone," reads a sign on the roof of a Rangoon jail. The message was hastily painted by Allied prisoners of war to prevent RAF aircraft from bombing the building. With the conflict in Burma at an end, the RAF undertook a final mission: flying Allied POWs back home again.

Acknowledgments

The index for this book was prepared by Gale Linck Partoyan. For their help with the preparation of this book, the editors also wish to thank: **In Australia:** Canberra—Australian War Memorial, Pictorial Department; Marguret Price, Australian Military History Researcher. **In France:** Paris—Cécile Coutin, Curator, Musée des Deux Guerres Mondiales; André Bénard, Odile Benoist, Elisabeth Bonhomme, Alain Degardin, Georges Delaleau, Gilbert Deloizy, Yvan Kayser, Général Pierre Lissarague, Director, Jean-Yves Lorent, Stéphane Nicolaou, Général Roger de Ruffray, Deputy Director, Colonel Pierre Willefert, Curator, Musée de l'Air; Saint-Léger-En-Yvelines—Peter Townsend; Vincennes—Patrick Facon, S.H.A.A. **In Great Britain:** Bracknell—Wing Commander D. Green, Royal Air Force Staff College; Cambridge—Constance Babington Smith; Cranwell—Jean M. King, Royal Air Force College; Hendon—A. C. Harold, R. W. Mack, P. Merton, M. Tagg, Alison Uppard, Royal Air Force Museum; Leicester—Squadron Leader H. Lees (Ret.); London—T. Graves; G. Clout, E. C. Hine, J. O. Simmonds, A. Williams, M. Willis, Imperial War Museum; G. Musgrove; Valerie Redmond; B. Robertson; Marjorie Willis, BBC Hulton Picture Library; Norwich—Chaz Bowyer; Uppingham—A. Price. **In India:** New Delhi—Group Captain Situ Mullick, AVSM. **In Italy:** Rome—Countess Maria Fede Caproni, Museo Aeronautico Caproni di Talideo; Nino Arena. **In New Zealand:** Auckland—Reg Coleman, Secretary, New Zealand Federation of Brevet Clubs; Christchurch—Squadron Leader John K. Barry, Director, Royal New Zealand Air Force Museum. **In the Republic of South Africa:** Johannesburg—Colonel D. Torlage, Museum of Natural History; Cecil William St. John Pattle. **In West Germany:** Koblenz—Marianne Loenartz, Meinrad Nilges, Bundesarchiv; Munich—Horst Amberg, Manager, Gemeinschaft der Jagdflieger; Hans Ring; Rösrath—Janusz Piekalkiewicz, Hoffnungsthal; West Berlin—Heidi Klein, Bildarchiv Preussischer Kulturbesitz.

Particularly useful sources of information and quotations used in this volume were *Enemy Coast Ahead* by Guy Gibson, Michael Joseph, London, 1946; *Battle Over Britain* by Francis K. Mason, Doubleday and Company, 1969; *The Nuremberg Raid 30-31 March 1944* by Martin Middlebrook, William Morrow and Company, 1974; *The Strategic Air Offensive Against Germany 1939-1945* by Charles Webster and Noble Frankland, Her Majesty's Stationery Office, London, 1961.

Bibliography

Books

Allen, H. R., *Who Won the Battle of Britain?* London: Arthur Barker, 1974.

Anderson, William, *Pathfinders.* London: Jarrolds Publishers, 1946.

Andrews, Allen, *The Air Marshals: The Air War in Western Europe.* William Morrow, 1970.

Baker, E. C. R., *The Fighter Aces of the R.A.F.* London: Kimber Paperback Library, 1962.

Barclay, George, *Fighter Pilot: A Self-portrait.* London: William Kimber, 1976.

Barker, Ralph:
   The Ship Busters: The Story of the R.A.F. Torpedo-Bombers. London: Chatto & Windus, 1957.
   Strike Hard, Strike Sure: Epics of the Bombers. London: White Lion Publishers, 1963.
   The Thousand Plane Raid. Ballantine Books, 1965.

Bekker, Cajus, *The Luftwaffe War Diaries.* London: MacDonald, 1966.

Bennett, D. C. T., *Pathfinder: A War Autobiography.* London: Sphere Books, 1972.

Bowyer, Chaz:
   For Valour: The Air VCs. London: William Kimber, 1978.
   Guns in the Sky: The Air Gunners of World War Two. Charles Scribner's Sons, 1978.

Bowyer, Michael J. F., *2 Group R.A.F.: A Complete History, 1936-1945.* London: Faber and Faber, 1979.

Brickhill, Paul, *Reach for the Sky: The Story of Douglas Bader, Legless Ace of the Battle of Britain.* W. W. Norton, 1954.

Charlton, L. E. O., *Britain at War: The Royal Air Force From April 1942 to June 1943.* London: Hutchinson, no date.

Churchill, Winston S., *The Second World War: Their Finest Hour.* Houghton Mifflin, 1949.

Collier, Basil:
   The Battle of Britain. MacMillan, 1962.
   The Defence of the United Kingdom. London: Her Majesty's Stationery Office, 1957.
   Leader of the Few: The Authorised Biography of Air Chief Marshal The Lord Dowding of Bentley Priory. London: Jarrolds, 1957.

Deere, Alan C., *Nine Lives.* London: Hodder & Stoughton, 1959.

Deighton, Len:
   Battle of Britain. London: George Rainbird, 1980.
   Fighter: The True Story of the Battle of Britain. Alfred A. Knopf, 1978.

Douglas, Sholto:
   Combat and Command: The Story of an Airman in Two World Wars. Simon and Schuster, 1963.
   Years of Command: The Second Volume of the Autobiography of Sholto Douglas. London: Collins, 1966.

Gibson, Guy, *Enemy Coast Ahead.* London: Michael Joseph, 1946.

Green, William, *Famous Fighters of the Second World War.* Doubleday, 1957.

Harris, Arthur, *Bomber Offensive.* London: Collins, 1947.

Hastings, Max, *Bomber Command.* Dial Press/James Wade, 1979.

Higham, Robin, *Air Power: A Concise History.* St. Martin's Press, 1972.

Information, Ministry of, *The Air Battle of Malta.* London: His Majesty's Stationery Office, 1944.

Irving, David, *The Rise and Fall of the Luftwaffe: The Life of Field Marshal Erhard Milch.* Little, Brown, 1973.

Jackson, Robert:
   Air War Over France May-June 1940. London: Ian Allan, 1974.
   Before the Storm: The Story of Royal Air Force Bomber Command 1939-42. London: Arthur Barker, 1972.

Lawrence, W. J., *No. 5 Bomber Group R.A.F. (1939-1945).* London: Faber and Faber, 1951.

Lewin, Ronald, *Churchill as Warlord.* Stein and Day, 1973.

Lloyd, Hugh Pughe, *Briefed to Attack: Malta's Part in African Victory.* London: Hodder & Stoughton, 1949.

Mason, Francis K., *Battle Over Britain.* Doubleday, 1969.

Mason, Timothy, *Leads the Field: The History of No. 12 Squadron Royal Air Force.* Lincoln, 1960.

Middlebrook, Martin, *The Nuremberg Raid 30-31 March 1944.* William Morrow, 1974.

Partridge, Eric, ed., *A Dictionary of Forces' Slang 1939-1945.* Books for Libraries Press, 1948.

Poolman, Kenneth, *Faith, Hope and Charity: Three Planes Against an Air Force.* London: Kimber, 1954.

Price, Alfred:
   Battle of Britain: The Hardest Day 19 August 1940. London: MacDonald and Jane's, 1979.
   Battle Over the Reich. Charles Scribner's Sons, 1973.

Richards, Denis, *The Fight at Odds.* London: Her Majesty's Stationery Office, 1974.

Richards, Denis, and Hilary St. George Saunders:
   The Fight Avails. London: Her Majesty's Stationery Office, 1975.

Rumpf, Hans, *The Bombing of Germany.* London: White Lion Publishers Limited, 1963.

Saundby, Robert, *Air Bombardment: The Story of its Development.* London: Chatto & Windus, 1961.

Saunders, Hilary St. George: *The Fight is Won.* London: Her Majesty's Stationery Office, 1975.

Tantum, W. H., IV and E. J. Hoffschmidt, eds., *The Rise and Fall of the German Air Force (1933 until 1945).* WE Inc., 1969.

Tedder, Arthur William, *With Prejudice: The War Memoirs of Marshal of the Royal Air Force Lord Tedder G.C.B.* Little, Brown, 1966.

Thetford, Owen, *Aircraft of the Royal Air Force Since 1918.* London: Putnam, 1957.

Thompson, H. L., *New Zealanders with the Royal Air Force: Vol. 3, Mediterranean and Middle East, South-east Asia.* Wellington: War History Branch, Department of Internal Affairs, 1959.

Townsend, Peter, *Duel of Eagles.* Simon and Schuster, 1970.

Verrier, Anthony, *The Bomber Offensive.* Macmillan, 1968.

Webster, Charles, and Noble Frankland, *The Strategic Air Offensive Against Germany 1939-1945.* London: Her Majesty's Stationery Office, 1961.

Wood, Derek, and Derek Dempster, *The Narrow Margin: The Battle of Britain and the Rise of Air Power 1930-40.* Greenwood Press, 1961.

Wright, Robert, *Dowding and the Battle of Britain.* London: Macdonald, 1969.

Ziegler, Frank, *The Story of 609 Squadron: Under the White Rose.* London: Macdonald, 1971.

Picture credits

The sources for the illustrations are shown below. Credits from left to right are separated by semicolons, from top to bottom by dashes. Endpaper (and cover detail, regular edition): Painting by Frank Wootton, England. 6, 7: Wide World. 8, 9: Popperfoto, London; BBC Hulton Picture Library, London. 10, 11: Popperfoto, London. 12, 13: Fox Photos, Ltd., London; insert, Wide World. 14, 15: BBC Hulton Picture Library, London. 16, 17: Via Musée de l'Air, Paris. 19: BBC Hulton Picture Library, London. 21: Courtesy Vickers, London—Flight International, Sutton, England. 22, 23: Vickers, courtesy Chaz Bowyer, Norwich, England; BBC Hulton Picture Library, London (2). 24: Imperial War Museum, London. 26: Painting by Michael Turner, Harrow, Middlesex, England. 27: The Auckland Collection, St. Albans, England. 31-33: Imperial War Museum, London. 34, 35: UPI. 38, 39: A painting in the Imperial War Museum, London, *Withdrawal From Dunkirk,* by Charles Cundall, No. LD305. 40-45: Drawings by John Batchelor. 46: Imperial War Museum, London. 48: A painting in the Imperial War Museum, London, *Air Chief Marshal Sir Hugh Dowding,* by Sir Walter Russell, No. LD1904. 49: Imperial War Museum, London. 50: Map by Walter Roberts. 53: Imperial War Museum, London. 54, 55: Imperial War Museum, London; Royal Air Force Museum, Hendon, England—A painting in the Imperial War Museum, London, *No. 11 Fighter Group's Operations Room, Uxbridge,* by Charles Cundall, No. LD4140. 56, 57: From *The Battle of Britain Then and Now,* edited by Winston G. Ramsey, © *After The Battle* magazine, 1980. 60, 61: A painting in the Imperial War Museum, London, *Air Fight Over Portland,* by Richard Eurich, No. LD769. 62: Imperial War Museum, London. 66: Fox Photos, Ltd., London; John Topham Picture Library, Endenbridge, Kent, England—Fox Photos, Ltd., London. 68: A painting in the Imperial War Museum, London, *A Good Landing is One You Can Walk Away From,* by Bill Hooper, No. LD6012. 70: Fox Photos, Ltd., London. 72, 73: National Archives Photo No. 306 NT 2743v. 74, 75: Imperial War Museum, London. 76, 77: Courtesy Chaz Bowyer, Norwich, England—courtesy Gerhard Schöpfel, Bergisch Gladbach, Germany. 78, 79: Popperfoto, London—Imperial War Museum, London. 80, 81: Bundesarchiv, Koblenz. 82: A painting in the Imperial War Museum, London, *Take Off,* by Laura Knight, No. LD3834. 84: Imperial War Museum, London. 87: Painting by Terence Cuneo, courtesy Sir George Edwards, Guildford, England. 89: Imperial War Museum, London. 91: Australian War Memorial, Canberra, No. 128221. 92, 93: Imperial War Museum, London. 94, 95: A painting in the Imperial War Museum, London, *Stirling Bomber Aircraft, Take-Off at Sunset,* by Charles Cundall, No. LD1849. 96: Imperial War Museum, London. 97: Map by Walter Roberts. 98: Derek Bayes, courtesy Royal Air Force Museum, Hendon, England. 102: Bundesarchiv, Koblenz. 104, 105: Drawing by John Batchelor—Fox Photos, Ltd., London; Australian War Memorial, Canberra, No. 3509. 106-110: Imperial War Museum, London. 111: Map by Walter Roberts. 114-119: Imperial War Museum, London. 121-124: William Vandivert for *Life.* 126, 127: Squadron Leader E. Welch, courtesy Chaz Bowyer, Norwich, England. 128, 129: Imperial War Museum, London. 130-135: Drawings by John Batchelor. 136, 137: Popperfoto, London. 138: Imperial War Museum, London. 139: Frank Scherschel for *Life.* 140-141: Map by Walter Roberts—drawing by Frederic F. Bigio from B-C Graphics; Imperial War Museum, London (2). 142: Imperial War Museum, London. 143: Painting by Michael Turner, Harrow, Middlesex, England. 146: © Hans Schaller, courtesy Ralph Barker, Caterham, England. 149: Imperial War Museum, London. 150: Central Press Photos, London—Cecil William St. John Pattle, Johannesburg, South Africa—Imperial War Museum, London. 151: Courtesy Chaz Bowyer, Norwich, England—Royal New Zealand Air Force, Wellington—Imperial War Museum, London. 152: British Official, courtesy Chaz Bowyer, Norwich, England—Imperial War Museum, London. 154: Imperial War Museum, London. 155: A painting in the Imperial War Museum, London, *Rocket-Firing Typhoons at the Falaise Gap, Normandy, 1944,* by Frank Wootton, No. LD4756. 157: Imperial War Museum, London. 160: Derek Bayes, painting by Gerald Coulson, courtesy Royal Air Force College, Cranwell, England. 162, 163: DPA, Frankfurt, Germany. 164, 165: Armed Forces Film and Photo Division, Ministry of Defense, India. 166, 167: Imperial War Museum, London. 168, 169: Armed Forces Film and Photo Division, Ministry of Defense, India. 170, 171: Imperial War Museum, London.

Index